THE JEWISH JESUS

THE
JEWISH
JESUS

Robert Aron

Translated by Agnes H. Forsyth
and Anne-Marie de Commaille,
and in collaboration with Horace T. Allen, Jr.

ORBIS BOOKS
MARYKNOLL, NEW YORK

Originally published in 1968 as *Ansi priait Jésus enfant*
by Editions Bernard Grasset, Paris.

TABLE OF CONTENTS

ABBREVIATIONS

ADPB   *The Authorized Daily Prayer Book.* Revised edition by Dr. Joseph H. Hertz (New York: Bloch Publishing Company, 1961).

SOS   *Service of the Synagogue,* edited by Dr. Hermann Adler, third edition (London: George Routledge and Sons Ltd., 1906).

Foreword

by the Rev. Horace T. Allen, Jr.

By its IMAGINATIVE and extended reconstruction of the spirituality and folk-religion within which Jesus grew to maturity, this timely book not only brings unique insight to the question of Christ and our time, but provides Jewish-Christian dialogue with practical content and suggestive theological interpretations. For any reader of the Christian Gospels, Robert Aron's description of the concrete circumstances of Jesus' early humanity, the daily and weekly course of life and prayer in Nazareth, and the annual solemnities in Jerusalem will be of no little help both to prayer and to understanding. His careful placing of Jesus within his Jewish heritage should create a helpful sense of identification and interest for those who still live within that tradition.

This volume also speaks directly to an increasingly significant theological preoccupation of our day: that of a concern with anthropology, with man "come of age," with the biblical affirmation of man in his maturity, as partner in creation and redeemed by the presence of God's word in man's world. Thus in describing the significance of the rite of *Bar Mitzvah*, Aron points out that "in Israel, which represents humanity, one can be a priest only if one is fully a man" (p. 150). Just as this falls sharply upon the ear of a Western Christian who is used to thinking of priesthood as something apart from or transcending manhood, so does Aron's emphasis upon the spiritual formation of the man, Jesus, strike an unusually contemporary theological note.

Finally and more generally, there is an interesting distinction throughout this book between the somewhat mystical and ritualistic "religion" of the Jewish Temple with its sacrificial system, and the more earthy, communal, "secular" faith expressed in the "world of benedictions" of the synagogue, in Jesus' Nazareth. Here, therefore, is yet another attempt to describe biblical faith, in the phrase of a contemporary Christian theologian, as "religionless." As Aron develops and analyzes the immediacy of the sacred to such a faith, one glimpses a new (and perhaps also, old) way of handling the traditional dichotomy of immanence and transcendence, in which these categories are not exclusive of one another but interpenetrating.

But even more important than these contemporary theological suggestions is the way in which this anthology of prayer and liturgy lights up the life and ministry of this mature man of God, the Jewish Jesus. If one needed an independent witness to the significance of such a study, it could perhaps be found in a profoundly moving passage in a Holy Week lecture given in 1958 by Dr. Olive Wyon. Speaking of Jesus' final "word" from the cross, "Father, into thy hands I commend my spirit," she observed,

> After one more "loud cry" — of thankful achievement — with the sigh of a contented child after a long day, Jesus bowed his head and breathed his soul into the Father's hands. He must have learned this prayer from his mother when he was a little boy at Nazareth, and now he falls asleep in his Father's arms (The Grace of the Passion by Olive Wyon, SCM Press, Ltd., London, 1959, pp. 22-23).

Robert Aron recreates for us the world of Nazareth's prayers and blessings so that we Jews and Christians together may learn anew how to bless our own world with Nazareth's Truth.

Union Theological Seminary
Passover Easter, 1970

Introduction

THIS BOOK WAS BEGUN as a sequel to *The Hidden Years of Jesus* and was intended to supplement it with the texts of prayers from the time of Jesus. It was to be an anthology by which Christians and Jews could become acquainted with the blessings, prayers and psalms used by Jesus in Nazareth and during his first journey to Jerusalem.

But books take their own course: *Habent sua fata libelli.* Topics do not always remain quietly within the framework provided for them. Very soon it became clear that to write a purely documentary book about Israel or Jesus would be impossible.

Our ancestors would have said that God is always the inner dynamic in any attempt to depict his people or individuals whom he brings into his covenant. In our quest for new certainties, our concern to discover afresh what our forebears had received through tradition, we find that everything related to Israel and Jesus in Israel is pregnant with problems which tor-

ment modern man and which will surely have to be solved
some day.

In gathering together these ancient prayer texts which are so
expressive of fundamental needs of Western culture, we suddenly realized that hidden in them were possible answers to
these anxieties and questions of our age of uncertainty.

These prayers are authentic witnesses to the significant
moment in which Christianity, however reluctantly, finally
separated itself from its Jewish origins. These texts, which
were supposed to be merely objective documents, suddenly
took on new life. The Jewish prayers of Jesus were anchored in
the strict and precise tradition of his ancestors and preserved
intact the tradition of Israel. Later they were transformed by
the disciples of Jesus: the *Kaddish*, for instance, is echoed in
the "Our Father." Texts from the Torah of Moses, and other
Old Testament sources were taken up and commented upon in
the apostolic books of the New Testament. Jewish customs
appear in the Gospel narrative from Nativity to Golgotha.
Without them one can understand neither the journey to the
Temple nor the Last Supper at Jerusalem, nor even the drama
of the Passion. Jewish rites for the reading of the Law and the
wearing of prayer shawls, Jesus' words and ritual gestures, so
often not understood by non-Jews or those ignorant of synagogue ritual, are all contained in the prayers of the young
Jesus and in his life in Israel. Israel seems to have survived
persecution and trial to help the religions which arose from it
to recover the purity of their own origin, as a foreshadowing
of their future.

So the young Jesus of 2,000 years ago prayed in an ancient
framework of faith. Did he perhaps anticipate in his petitions
the present crisis wherein all sense of the sacred and of the
divine is in danger of being lost?

But Israel has always been for the faithful Jew a tangible and
unquestioned reality. The Jew does not "believe" in God in
the way in which we use that word; he is directly aware of the
presence of God. If he is a nonbeliever, he experiences his

nonpresence. The Jew needs certainty: it is not enough for him merely to "believe."

Ancient Hebrew, in Jesus' day the language of prayer, has no word to denote "belief" as we understand it today. There is, however, a word, *Emuna*, which implies certainty. It has for its root, *Amn*, which can be pronounced *amen*. For Jews and Christians alike those three letters indicate the consent of the faithful to the will of God. Although the term is the same before and after Jesus, the meaning has changed. For the Jew of Jesus' time, *amen* traditionally expressed a statement of fact. For many believers today for whom religious experience is less immediate and direct, *amen* is a wish, a hope, an aspiration. In our day *amen* often means "so be it." To the ancient Jew, the syllables meant "so it is." The ministry of Jesus marks the turning point between these two meanings: between the existential one of the religion of Israel and the expectant one of modern belief.

How then did the God of Israel reveal himself to his ancient people? How did he approach them in the midst of their human existence, this God who made his presence felt in so immanent a way in the world as to transform it from within?

In the Torah we find in the beginning neither a theological affirmation nor a metaphysical description of the divine qualities: God's greatness, his strength or his kindness. He is God, the Creator of the world, and this is all-inclusive. He permits man to discover his attributes one by one and to benefit by them. In the first basic words of the Decalogue, in the first affirmation of his existence before the assembled people, what does he say? Just one fact, a fact that the assembled Hebrews affirmed: "I am Yahweh your God; I brought you out of the land of Egypt, out of the house of bondage" (Ex. 20: 1-2).

To this, the people answered with one voice, simply acknowledging the fact: "You are the Lord our God who brought us out of the land of Egypt."

Nothing more. It is simple as the truth, simple as the obvious. It is undeniable, irrefutable — and fundamentally Jewish.

Later, when God wants to define himself through his attributes, he will select that of his own self-evident existence: *Ehyé acher ehyé*, "I am that I am." Once again, it is undeniable, irrefutable.

Such then is the direct and living relationship between the Jew and his God. If he does not "believe" in him in the ordinary sense of the word, it is because he does not need to believe, since he is directly aware of his presence.

The prayers of the young Jesus, as we shall see, are filled with this existential certainty. They are rooted in the physical and not in the mystical world. They are rooted in the world of God's presence and not in faith in his presence. These prayers are linked to everyday living and not to transfigurations and sacrifices which may exalt and sanctify but which may also disfigure reality.

The prayers of the young Jesus are not supplications but actions accompanying concrete facts. In our time, which is so fond of objective truth, when materialism is so attractive, and both man and God are in question, let us listen to Jesus at prayer and try in that way to rediscover with him a path towards the God of truth.

To pray with the young Jesus, to rediscover the point of his prayers, is perhaps to rediscover the real meaning of our own destiny. Perhaps then the "so be it" *amen* will be united with the "so it is" *amen*. And together men of both Testaments may repeat with one voice: *amen*.

In the history of Israel and of all that has flowed from it, including belief and nonbelief, the evolution of the "so it is" *amen* to the "so be it" *amen* began at Sinai. Indeed, for Israel and for the children of Abraham all subsequent relations with God were established at Sinai in a procedure readily understood by the most secular of our contemporaries since it strangely resembles the modern way of voting.

First of all, God, speaking through his delegate Moses, made sure that he would have a "quorum" present. Thus he gathered around the mountain the thousands of Hebrews he had brought out of Egypt so that they could give him a majority, even unanimity. He asked for a vote of confidence; he proposed a referendum in which the people would have to decide, and which would involve not only their immediate future but also their eternal destiny: "Do you agree to be a kingdom of priests and a holy nation?"

That question included all the troubles and all the opportunities of Israel, all the persecutions that men would inflict upon it and all the benefits they would expect from it, all its apostasy and repentant faith—a strange question when addressed to a people who were in no way prepared for priesthood. Not one of those faced with this decision could escape it; they had to say "yes" or "no."

So God risks all. Will chaos ensue, challenging creation and destroying the Covenant, or will men be consecrated to God in spite of centuries of forgetfulness and denial? With one voice the assembled people answered "yes," *naassé vehischma*. God had won.

The second step at Sinai consists of the moral code which God gave the people, the ten basic words called the "ten commandments," which constitute the Decalogue. These are not detailed instructions but general directions that are easily understood. The Lord began by reminding the Jews of his goodness to them, of his divine intervention: "I am Yahweh your God who brought you out of the land of Egypt, out of the house of bondage."

Then come nine commands: two of them positive, indicating what must be done, and the other seven negative, outlining both the religious attitude of the chosen people ("You shall have no gods except me; you shall make no idols. Remember the Sabbath Day and keep it holy"), and the secular code of morals which will govern all men (not to kill, not to covet, not to commit adultery . . .).

Then follows the third step, which includes all the corollaries of these principles: the 613 obligations, 365 negative and 248 positive, which will from then on and for all eternity guide the behavior of the Jews and manifest in the life of each one—if he is a practicing believer—the priesthood accepted at Sinai. These innumerable and overwhelming specifications would probably have seemed impossible of attainment by the majority of the Hebrews gathered around the mountain. But this elaboration did not appear until a later time when, according to tradition, the Lord revealed it to Moses who then codified the rules governing the priesthood of the people chosen by God.

And so it is that God formed his Covenant with Israel in a modern, secular fashion, following the procedure of a parliament. It was neither the first nor the last of these *berit*, of these successive covenants that became milestones in the divine revelation, that is, the progressive grasping by human intelligence of what can be known of God and what God chooses to reveal. For example, there was the initial covenant with Adam, which in its elementary simplicity involved obedience to the Lord. We know what came of that. There was the covenant of the rainbow with Noah, the most ecumenical and bold of all, made without distinction of person, kind, race, belief or unbelief, with all that lived upon the face of the earth. There was the covenant with Abraham, which made of him the first missionary, shaping his life in obedience to the sharp order to abandon the normal setting of his life for the service of God: *Lekh, lekha*—"Go, depart." None of these covenants was annulled by Sinai for nothing can annul a covenant once concluded. Each covenant is complete in itself and corresponds simply to a different moment of eternity all of whose moments have equal value. But the covenant of Sinai is unique and especially compelling to all generations and nations of the world in that it dedicates to priesthood a people prepared for it only through the persecution undergone during its captivity in Egypt. The priests so invested have not come from seminaries but from ghettos and extermination camps where their firstborn were killed.

These people were ordinary people: virtuous and wicked,

believers and those who were ready to worship the golden calf, good men who were inclined to observe every word of the moral code and others who were ready to compromise and cut corners.

All that can be found in the human heart, all that torments man in his flesh, tempts his reason or provokes him to folly, all tendencies, good and bad, which will always be part of the human condition, are present at Sinai. As Deuteronomy says: "Not with you alone do I make this covenant today and pronounce these sanctions, but with him also who is not here today as well as with him who stands with us here in the presence of Yahweh our God" (Dt.29:13-15).

The young Jesus, like every Jewish child, is therefore present at Sinai. For years he will stay hidden in the womb of history, waiting for the moment when the will of God calls him forth to appear before the world.

He was present at Sinai. He is to be present to all the world. Moses precedes him, and he follows Moses. The possibility of such interrelationship has been suggested by the famous *Midrash* of Rabbi Akiba, on Moses' vision at Sinai. Let us expound that *Midrash* here as a justification for our own study of the Jewish prayers of Jesus.

When Moses is at Sinai bringing the Law to the Hebrews, suddenly, at a particular instant in that exceptional place, he has an extraordinary vision which broadens his perception to encompass the whole world and the span of the centuries. Scattered all over the earth and at each stage of history, he sees men who in their own languages, according to their own customs and beliefs, ceaselessly add their commentaries to his revelation. To each of his words they add mountains of exegesis and successive waves of interpretation. Surprised to see his words extending in time and space, he is still more surprised to note as he listens, that they are returning to him in languages and meanings which he himself does not understand. His descendants are a mystery to him; traditions stemming from him are foreign to him. Shall he reject them? In this strange moment in which all human progress with its diversity and contradiction seems to resound in his ears and defy his intelligence, Moses hesitates. What path should he take? On his choice will depend the future of man and God. Finally he makes up his mind. Realizing that all these human paraphrases of the revealed word are linked to him and to God and wondering that his own words have given birth to so many commentaries related directly to him, he solemnly declares himself to be in agreement with all those who acknowledge him as their spiritual father, even though he does not understand them. He endorses the unknown progress of man. And because he is not alone at Sinai, "but with him also who is not here today," he is joined by all those who will witness to the covenant, believers and nonbelievers alike, and by those who are accepted or rejected by the Jewish religion. There, too, present at Sinai is Jesus.

What Jesus brings to the covenant of Sinai perhaps alters the early religion; it is nonetheless one of those commentaries which life always has the right to add to the eternal Word, thus adapting it to history's diversity and contradiction.

This book has been written from that point of view.

The prayers of the young Jesus, still bound to the traditions of his fathers, would in no way surprise Moses. They still conform to his teaching; they are still purely Jewish. But, perhaps, in the course of this book, it will become possible for us to notice innovations and changes. Perhaps we shall see how, little by little, the "so it is" *amen*, which is the *amen* of the people assembled at Sinai, has changed its meaning and has become the "so be it" *amen*, which today ends many of our prayers.

And so we may perhaps be able to detect in the history of God a change of direction which was begun during the hidden years of Jesus, the consequences of which have yet to be seen.

Leolam vahed, in saecula saeculorum, What does God's future hold? There lies the whole question.

1. His Birth and Childhood

So Joseph set out . . . and travelled up to Judaea, to the town
of David called Bethlehem . . . and she gave birth to a son, her
first-born (Lk. 2:4-7).

FROM THE VERY MOMENT of his birth a Jewish child of Jesus' day
was linked in a special way to his land. His birth was not just
another moment in the continuity of family or another bond
strengthening the love of his parents. Nor was it only a civil
event whereby a new name was inscribed upon the rolls of so-
ciety. A birth was even more than a new bridge towards the
uncertainties of the future.

The birth of a child, a physical and human event, added new
strength to the spiritual forces which had made the land of
Palestine the most biblical of biblical lands. It was the Jewish
vision that there were no secular places or events untouched
by the outpouring of the Spirit. Every contour of the land,
every village of Palestine where was born that child of unique

9

destiny, was shaped by the Spirit. There, every act was full of
meaning, every place a place of destiny, every man an indis-
pensable link in the continuing presence of spiritual power. So
the universe was filled with Spirit, the world sacred, and the
Lord everywhere present. It is not only history that may be
spoken of as sacred, but also the topography and geography of
the land of Jesus' birth — a land of benediction and of religion.

Not even Jerusalem, the capital of that land, or the Temple at
its heart, could claim such identification with the religion of
Israel. For it was the tendency of the Temple to paralyze
religion, precisely as too many clerics and theologians tend to
hinder rather than to serve the purposes of God.

Let us turn to the Talmud, to both Talmuds. The Talmud of
Jerusalem was written down in the fourth century A.D., and the
Talmud of Babylon in the fifth century; both of them are commentaries on that of Judah the Prince, who about the year 200
recorded the oral tradition and the opinions and interpretations of distinguished teachers, including those who were contemporary with Jesus. These interpretations and discussions
formed a commentary on the Law, applying it to daily life and
to the changing course of history.

The Talmud, which mirrors the Jewish spirit at the time of
the Second Temple, describes in a very singular fashion the
geography of Palestine in Jesus' day. It makes no attempt at
topographical accuracy. It reflects neither a physical nor political nor economic geography, but what might be called "theological" geography, or more exactly, "religious" geography.
Just as the Gothic cathedrals of the Middle Ages have been
called "stone bibles" because of the mysticism and symbolism
of their arches, their sculptured portals and their stained glass,
recalling the great religious themes of the two Testaments, one
can even more logically refer to the very soil of Palestine as an
"earthen bible," interpreted and even transfigured by the spirituality of Israel and the will of God.

One of the most usual names for Palestine, therefore, was
Eretz Israel, "The Land of Israel." It was the land of all lands.

All other lands not so dedicated to the worship of God were called "outside the land," meaning either secular or godless, as the case might be. It was just the opposite in the case of Roman boundaries, which were mapped out according to political or military need. The Jews, however, fixed no boundaries between themselves and the neighboring regions. They described their country, according to whether given towns and districts practiced the religion of Israel or some idolatrous cult.

This system was carried on by the apostles of Jesus, who were molded by Judaism and were therefore more conversant with the Jewish divisions of Palestine than with Caesar's. For instance, a city on the coast of Samaria, Caesarea, was regarded by the Romans as part of Palestine, but the Talmud excluded it because of its unfaithfulness to certain prescriptions of the Law. Following this same Jewish point of view, in the Acts of the Apostles it is declared a foreign city.

And so the land of Palestine, this land of all lands, was filled with the divine and shaped by sacred history. Contemporary rabbinical tradition described specific aspects of the land in the following way: there were three springs in Palestine, one at Tiberias, one at Abilene and one at the cave of Panéas. Supposedly they arose after the Flood. When the waters subsided they were still visible in the ground as if to commemorate, along with the rainbow, the covenant made by God with all living creatures. No less than three springs were needed to irrigate man's earth with the water that sanctified it, to consecrate to the service of humanity the waters that had nearly destroyed it. Actually only the first of these springs exists today. One wonders what became of the other two, for there is no trace of them. Did they dry up, or did they exist only in the imagination of rabbis who felt that the divine mercy should be manifested simultaneously in several parts of this predestined land?

When the Talmudists enumerate the seas or lakes in Palestine, they also come up with seven, although in reality there are only six. Seven, of course, is the Bible's favorite number.

And so the teachers who were contemporaries of Jesus cared very little about accuracy in recording the geography of their country. What counted as far as they were concerned, and what they would teach is that the land of Palestine formed a tight web of symbolic legend and religious precept.

For instance, Rabbi Eliezer, a Talmudic rabbi, tells of his father's goats in the Machaerus mountains of Peraea. He declares that they fattened on nothing more than the smell of incense prepared in the Temple—thirty miles away across the Dead Sea—an anecdote that should neither be taken literally nor recommended to the peasants of Palestine as a means of feeding their flocks!

There are other such legends. One of them tells about the most famous of the valleys in Palestine, the valley of Josaphat, where, according to the prophets, God will judge his people. All speak of it and believe they know it. The only drawback is simply that it has never existed. It is an imaginary place, but such imagination is more pregnant with meaning than many a reality.

Still another legend of the Talmud of Babylon gives a mythical origin to the people of Palestine. According to Rabbi Eliezer, son of Rabbi José the Galilean: "It is the dead that Ezekiel brought to life who went to Palestine, married and had children." Thus were the Jewish people rooted in earliest antiquity and in their unique vocation.

In the Temple at Jerusalem in the Holy of Holies there was a stone a few inches high called "the foundation stone." In the era of the First Temple, the Ark of the Covenant rested on it, and in Jesus' day at *Yom Kippur*, the Day of Atonement, the high priest placed on it the incense of sacrifice. In the imagination of the authors of the Talmud this stone of stones took on a symbolic value which transcended its actual use. In their minds it became the foundation stone of the whole earth.

Yom Kippur gave rise to other parabolic symbolism. Jericho, which lies near the Jordan River and the Dead Sea, is the key to Palestine. "If we capture Jericho," said the Jews during their struggle with the kings of Canaan, "the whole country will be ours." It is a city of exceptional strategic value, a green and fragrant city which in Deuteronomy and Judges is called "the city of palm trees." But more importantly it bore an almost supernatural relationship to the Temple at Jerusalem, such that the Talmud could say, "The voice of the high priest was heard in Jericho," when on *Yom Kippur* he recited the Tetragram in the Temple at Jerusalem. And further, "The odor of the incense burnt in the Temple reached Jericho on that day." The fact that the distance between the two cities is seventeen miles is irrelevant to the symbolism whereby they become neighbors and twins.

A whole imaginary web of interpretation and belief is thus added to the countryside in order to define its vocation. But legends or parables were not the only means of expressing the spirituality of the land of Palestine. There were also religious customs in Jesus' time which consecrated to God and to the observance of his Law, fields, orchards and towns which otherwise would have been mere parcels of soil or assorted structures. Like Teilhard de Chardin in the desert celebrating a "Mass on the World" whose altar was the whole world, so the Jews of Palestine, in order to worship, sought out places where nature and the Law met and where the land was transformed by the Spirit of the Lord.

For example, the Law required that one day in the week be devoted to rest and to the study of the Torah: the Sabbath, which begins at nightfall on Friday evening and lasts till dusk on Saturday. Why should the land of Palestine, consecrated to God, not conform to that law? Why should its rivers not conform to the teachings of the Torah? Why should the rivers not be "pure" or "impure" and why would the pure ones, the most holy and best adapted to the service of God, not comply with rules of the Sabbath? A whole religious hierarchy is thus established among the rivers which flow through Palestine. The Jordan, the largest, is from a religious point of view, of questionable orthodoxy. The Talmud marvels on the one hand that its waters do not mix with the waters of the Lake of Tiberias as it flows through it. Is this because it must remain pure? On the other hand, a little farther on, after it has left the lake, the Jordan is joined by a tributary, the Yarmuk, almost as large. The *Mishnah* declares that, from that point on, their waters may not be used in the Temple since both have been contaminated.

The same applies to two other rivers, the Kermion and the Figa, whose muddied waters could not serve for the sacrifices. And so the observance of the Law was no easier for rivers than it was for men. Just as Israel was always oscillating between strict observance of its priestly mission and forgetfulness of it, so its land was watered by rivers which were sometimes pure and sometimes impure.

Fortunately, we come now to a river about whose extraordinary destiny there is no doubt: the Sambation, the "sabbatical river," whose waters flow rapidly during the week and stop on the Sabbath. This has been recorded—with some variations—by both secular and sacred authors, by Pliny in his *Natural History*, and by rabbis in the *Midrash*.

So a river with an intermittent flow of waters existed in *Eretz Israel*, in "The Land of Israel." Flavius Josephus, the Jewish historian, almost a contemporary of Jesus, records it, too, but he reverses the times of drought and of flood, stating that the sabbatical river flows only on the seventh day. Today, Moslems who have also noticed the river and its irregular flow, agree with Josephus rather than with Pliny and the Talmud. According to them, the Nahr-el-Arus flows only one day a week and the river-flow occurs not on Saturday but on Friday, their traditional day of rest.

Thus the Semitic spirit, the Jewish imagination, plays upon material facts. The universe becomes an interweaving of symbols or parables. Everyone in it, by the very fact of his birth, shares in this intimate presence of God in nature and finds himself surrounded by the world as God's creation.

Let us take another example, not of the Sabbath day this

time, but of the sabbatical year. Every seventh year is a year of
rest and requires that the Jews allow the ground to lie fallow in
order that it may replenish its reserves. During that year vege-
tation grows wild and from spring to winter freely bears its
leaves, flowers and fruit according to the cycle of the seasons,
no longer interrupted or warped by the needs of men.

This rest is not only beneficial to the land and a means of
maintaining its fertility, but is nature's celebration of the Sabbath. It, too, returns to the Lord, to its Creator, in accordance
with the natural rhythm initiated in Genesis. So it is that the
seven years, like the seven days of the week, lead to the same
celebration and transformation. Time normally used for secular
activity recovers its sacred character. For the farmer, each Sabbath in this sabbatical year is even holier than usual. On those
days he is doubly in contact with the Lord: in his own right
and through his fields.

But man does live day by day as well as year by year. How
then is he to depend on soil which, one year out of seven,
yields no fruit? Undoubtedly he will have reserves put aside
for the sabbatical year and will obtain elsewhere what he cannot take from his own fields. But even so he must not cut himself off totally from the land in this special year of its celebration of the Law. How then will he assure his livelihood normally provided by the rhythm of the crops but which this year
must be interrupted?

It is on such an occasion that throughout Palestine, throughout *Eretz* one experiences the divine unity in terms both of
land and labor. It is as if the whole country made an effort to
replace the field that is allowed to lie fallow, as if the entire
land of Palestine made it possible for the owner of an idle field
to exist without transgressing the divine law to which both he
and his land are committed.

If man has to procure elsewhere the vegetables or fruit that
his fields no longer produce, he must do so only in a favorable
season prescribed by the law of the Lord. The *Biour*, a custom
which will be described much later by Maimonides, forbids

during the sabbatical year the eating of fruits that have fallen after those which are left on the trees have begun to dry. Here again it is the natural rhythm of life that must be respected. The application of this custom varies from country to country, since in some countries the fruit dries up sooner than in others.

In Palestine there are at least four towns which regulate the consumption of the three essential foods then in use. The first is Jericho. During the sabbatical year, an owner of Palestinian land consecrated to the Sabbath rest of the Lord has the right to eat dates only until the last ones are no longer seen on the streets of Jericho. In like manner consumption of olives is regulated from Meroth and Gousch Halab. And because Oubal (known also as Abel) is well known for its vineyards, the Talmud of Babylon declares, "One may eat grapes until those of the vineyards of Abel or Oubal have disappeared." In such a way does the sap that swells the vines in these orchard towns nourish the recurring cycle of religious life in Palestine.

There is another occasion when the land of Palestine plays a part in the ceremonies that note the passage of time. In the Temple of Jerusalem and in other Palestinian places of worship each month, the rising of the new moon is marked by a ceremony. In a time when clocks did not exist the whole country had to be alerted simultaneously. The Sanhedrin, the supreme authority in religious matters, gathered in Beth-Yaazek, a large courtyard at Jerusalem, when the expected moment was drawing near. There they awaited the word of those who would first see the new moon. The moment they came, the Sanhedrin fixed the date of the month and the date of feast days. Then the renewal of the month was announced to the provinces by means of fires lit on the surrounding hills. One of these hills, the Mount of Olives, was afterwards to become well known. Later on, the Samaritans, in their struggle with Judaea, purposely interfered by lighting similar fires in places and at times which led to great confusion. So the fires were suppressed in Judaea, and messengers hurried to the principal towns to announce the new month.

Another ritual of time was the morning sacrifice. Before the sacrifice was offered in the Temple at Jerusalem, according to the *Mishnah*, those charged with announcing the new day were asked whether it was light at Hebron. Hebron, south of Jerusalem in the mountains of Judaea, was touched by dawn earlier than the eastern plains. As soon as daybreak whitened its heights, the news was immediately carried to Jerusalem, and all was prepared so that at the moment the light reached the Temple the sacrifice could begin.

So the land where Jesus was born had a part in the ordering of the ritual to which it gave a material base and form. And men accepted it as the only intermediary between themselves and their Creator.

As a child of "The Land," one of its greatest, Jesus himself realized his earthly destiny in places especially known for their association with the winds of the Spirit. Twice, coming to these places of the Spirit, he is quickened by the power which he has already come to expect from them according to the tradition of his people. He will later translate these expectations to fit the needs of his disciples.

The first of these places is the Mount of Olives, the mountain top on which the fire was lit to announce the new cycle of the months.

The second is Mount Çouk, the famous Mount Azazel of the Bible from which the scapegoat was hurled to expiate the sins of Israel. It was ten days' walk from Jerusalem. The *Mishnah* says of this ritual: "Ten tents were set up from Jerusalem to Çouk. The man who led the scapegoat to the desert was accompanied as far as the last tent by the leading men of Jerusalem. In each of the tents he was offered food and water," as was fitting in a barren land. When the summit was reached, the goat was thrown into a precipice so jagged that he was broken to pieces before reaching the bottom.

This is the mountain where all the sins of Israel were abolished, the spot destined for expiation, tragic and murderous, demanding its ration of blood to cleanse humanity. According to Talmudists whose competence seems assured,

Mount Çouk is none other than the Mount of Temptation, Quarantinia, where, according to the Gospels, Jesus was tempted by the devil. Therefore, it is on this dramatic site where Israel felt the formidable impact of its religious vocation that Jesus lived through the first drama of his destiny.

During the ministry of Christ other places also repeated the roles they had long held in Jewish religion, for example, Tiberias and Golgotha. The Gospels inform us that Jesus avoided the city of Tiberias although he spent much time on the shores of its lake. This city, built on old tombs, was considered impure.

As for Golgotha, it is a rock in the shape of a skull situated above Jeremiah's cave near the spot where, according to Jewish tradition, execution by stoning used to take place.

Though the interpretations of these traditions have differed from time to time, we may assume that any Jewish prayer which in Jesus' time expressed the sacred character of "The Land" will also strike a responsive chord in the hearts of those who believe in the vocation of the young Palestinian Jew.

Among the prayers directly inspired by the land there is one, the prayer of the dew, which, though later than Jesus' time, expresses what has always been a topic of Jewish piety. We find this prayer at the "Additional Services" of Passover, perhaps not expressed in the same terms as before, but at least inspired by the same thought:

> *When, at the dawn of time, the Lord sought the right moment to create all things, he chose the season of the dew. . . .*

> *A blanket of dew moistened the Garden of Eden, and the regions above were the reservoir of this precious gift. The body of man was formed from the dust of the earth and animated by the breath of life, the divine dew. It was also from the dew that the earth received its fertility; through the dew it was covered with fruit and foliage. The rain had not yet fallen on the earth, so it was the dew which refreshed and gladdened it.*

> How sweet is the fortune reserved to it by the dew, for one
> day a celestial dew will revive those who sleep in its bosom.
>
> It is you, O Lord our God, who make the wind to blow and
> the dew to fall, for good and not for ill, to give us abundance
> and not want, life and not death.

How could a young Jew two thousand years ago, as he gave
thanks for the land of Israel and the source of its fertility, fail
to sense the destiny and charm of that country so filled with
the Spirit?

Into this sacred land whose every aspect recalls the service
of God, Jesus, like any other child, is introduced by custom
and by ceremony. The ritual surrounding his origin and birth
depends upon his family lineage and upon the faithfulness of
his parents to the tradition of Israel, and marks his inclusion
in the Covenant of God.

Let us look first at his ancestry which, according to the Gospels, is of the line of David, a line historically entrusted with a
special vocation.

In the present services of the synagogue there is a tradition
which may help us to understand by analogy what it meant at
the time of Jesus to belong to the lineage of David.

A kind of religious aristocracy continues among Jews today;
it is that of the *cohanim*.* They are members of families supposedly descended from the high priest Aaron, Moses'
brother, who was the first to exercise the priesthood. Through
the centuries his line continued, multiplied and scattered
throughout the different communities of Israel. Those who
belong to it have a special role in these services: the privilege,
for example, of pronouncing the divine blessing on the Sabbath, or on a weekday and on certain feastdays.

Except for this priestly function, the descendants of Aaron
differ in no way from other Jews. Some are rich; others are

Cohanim is the plural of the Hebrew word *cohen*, which means *"priest."*
Some Jews took it as their family name when they were granted civil status.

poor. Some are obviously devout; others seem totally unaware of their special dignity. But they are obliged to apply the Law in their daily lives more strictly than the rank and file of believers. *Cohanim* may not marry divorced women or proselytes too recently converted, and they may not approach the dead. They constitute a religious aristocracy which is neither an aristocracy of power nor of money, nor even necessarily of the spirit.

One may suppose that the descendants of David at the time of Jesus were in the same position as are the descendants of the high priest Aaron today. Both were aware of an inheritance that consecrated them to the service of God with no accompanying glory or privilege. No advantage, either social or material, resulted from belonging to such prestigious lineage. Surely there were among the descendants of King David those who were undistinguished personalities, financially, socially and intellectually. Yet there lived in each of them the pure tradition of Israel.

Joseph and Mary, as the Gospels tell us, were people of little means, but they were filled with Jewish spirituality. Both, through different lines, were descendants of David. The Gospels establish Joseph's genealogy thus:

> *Abraham was the father of Isaac,*
> *Isaac the father of Jacob,*
> *Jacob the father of Judah and his brothers,*

*   *   *   *   *

> *Boaz was the father of Obed, Ruth being his mother,*
> *Obed was the father of Jesse;*
> *and Jesse was father of King David.*

*   *   *   *   *

> *and Jacob was the father of Joseph the husband of Mary;*
> *of her was born Jesus who is called Christ (Mt. 1:1-16).*

> *When he started to teach, Jesus was about thirty years old,*
> *being the son, as it was thought, of Joseph son of*
> *Heli, . . . son of David . . . son of Isaac . . . son of Abra-*
> *ham . . . son of Seth, son of Adam, son of God (Lk.*
> *3:23-38).*

As for Mary, when we consult nonbiblical sources, some of
which are contemporary, and certain Fathers of the Church,
we find her Davidic lineage traced thus: her father, Joachim,
belonged to the tribe of Judah and to the family of David. Her
mother, Anne, had had from a first marriage with a certain
Clopas, a daughter whom the Gospel later called Mary of
Clopas. Ten years after the birth of her first child, Anne, who
was now the wife of Joachim, gave birth to Miriam or Mary
who is the mother of Jesus. Therefore, on the paternal side,
Jesus is from the line of David. Through her marriage to
Joseph, who was also a descendant of David, Mary brought to
the child Jesus a double consecration and a double tie with
this royal line.

The marriage of Mary and Joseph, celebrated according to
Jewish rite, had strengthened their attachment to the Law of
Israel.

Matrimony at that time included two states: the engagement
and the marriage itself. The engagement was a religious commitment and could be broken only by divorce.

When Joseph took Mary as his fiancée, he had made the
ritual promise of providing her with food, lodging and clothes.
A year later the marriage was celebrated in a service customary
at the time and described in the Talmud. Some of its features
are part of Jewish weddings today.

The fiancée was carried in on a palanquin, her hair floating
under a veil and golden ornaments on her forehead. Young
virgins "and the friends of the wedding" surrounded the pair,
throwing seeds along their way.

The bridegroom released the bride from any vows she might
have taken before her marriage. The oaths were then ex-
changed beneath a canopy called a *chuppah.*

When the moment of the nuptial blessings came, the celebrant took a cup full of wine and pronounced the following
verses:

> Blessed art thou, O Lord our God, King of the universe, who
> created the fruit of the vine.

> Blessed art thou, O Lord our God, King of the universe, who
> hast hallowed us by thy commandments, and hast given us
> command concerning forbidden marriages; who hast disal-
> lowed unto us those that are betrothed, but hast sanctioned
> unto us such as are wedded to us by the rite of the nuptial
> canopy and the sacred covenant of wedlock (ADPB, p. 1011).

The couple then drank a little of the wine blessed by the celebrant who, in Nazareth, might have been an inhabitant of the
village well versed in the divine service. When the bridegroom
placed the wedding ring on the bride's finger in the presence
of two witnesses, he said: "Behold, thou art consecrated unto
me by this ring, according to the Law of Moses and of Israel"
(Ibid.).

The celebrant then took a second cup of wine and recited the
seven following blessings, again beginning with the blessing
of the wine.

> Blessed art thou, O Lord our God, King of the universe, who
> createst the fruit of the vine.

*   *   *   *   *

> Blessed art thou, O Lord our God, King of the universe,
> Creator of man.

> Blessed art thou, O Lord our God, King of the universe, who
> hast made man in thine image, after thy likeness, and hast
> prepared unto him, out of his very self, a perpetual fabric.
> Blessed art thou, O Lord, Creator of man.

> May she who was barren (Zion) be exceeding glad and

exult, when her children are gathered within her in joy. Blessed art thou, O Lord, who makest Zion joyful through her children.

O make these loved companions greatly to rejoice, even as of old thou didst gladden thy creature in the garden of Eden. Blessed art thou, O Lord, who makest bridegroom and bride to rejoice.

Blessed art thou, O Lord our God, King of the universe, who hast created joy and gladness, bridegroom and bride, mirth and exultation, pleasure and delight, love, brotherhood, peace and fellowship. Soon there may be heard in the cities of Judah, and in the streets of Jerusalem, the voice of joy and gladness, the voice of the bridegroom and the voice of the bride, the jubilant voice of bridegrooms from their canopies, and of youths from their feasts of song. Blessed art thou, O Lord, who makest the bridegroom to rejoice with the bride (ADPB, p. 1013).

After these blessings he took a sip of the wine and asked the newlyweds to do the same; then he poured away what was left and broke the glass. This last is still done and has been explained in various ways: as a sign of joy, or, on the contrary, to remind one of the fall of the Temple of Jerusalem.

Finally the ceremony ended with the recitation of Psalm 45, to be said not only after the blessings but at the home of the newlyweds for seven successive days.

Here is the text of the psalm which the Jewish and Christian traditions interpret as the wedding song of the King-Messiah and his bride Israel:

My heart is stirred by a noble theme:
I address my poem to the king;
my tongue is ready as the pen of a busy scribe.

Of all men you are the most handsome,
your lips are moist with grace,
for God has blessed you for ever.

Hero, strap your sword at your side,
in majesty and splendour; on, ride on,
in the cause of truth, religion and virtue!

Stretch the bowstring tight,
lending terror to your right hand.
Your arrows are sharp; nations lie at your mercy,
the king's enemies are losing heart.

Your throne, God, shall last for ever and ever,
your royal sceptre is a sceptre of integrity:
virtue you love as much as you hate wickedness.

This is why God, your God, has anointed you
with the oil of gladness, above all your rivals;
myrrh and aloes waft from your robes.

From palaces of ivory harps entertain you,
daughters of kings are among your maids of honour;
on your right stands the queen, in gold from Ophir.

Listen, daughter, pay careful attention:
forget your nation and your ancestral home,
then the king will fall in love with your beauty.
He is your master now, bow down to him.

The daughter of Tyre will solicit your favour with gifts,
the wealthiest nations, with jewels set in gold.

Dressed in brocades, the king's daughter
is led in to the king, with bridesmaids in her train.

Her ladies-in-waiting follow
and enter the king's palace to general rejoicing.

Your ancestors will be replaced by sons
whom you will make lords of the whole world.

I shall immortalize your name,
nations will sing your praises for ever and ever
(Ps. 45; cf. Ezk. 16:8-13; Is. 62:5).

And so from the very beginning, the family into which Jesus was born was nurtured in the sacred atmosphere which would continue to surround him, and in which he would receive the sign of the Covenant before being purified with his mother. The Gospels give precise details on those rites:

> *When the eighth day came and the child was to be circumcised, they gave him the name Jesus, the name the angel had given him before his conception (Lk. 2:21).*

> *And when the day came for them to be purified as laid down by the Law of Moses, they took him up to Jerusalem to present him to the Lord — observing what stands written in the Law of the Lord:* Every first-born male must be consecrated to the Lord — *and also to offer in sacrifice, in accordance with what is said in the Law of the Lord,* a pair of turtledoves or two young pigeons *(Lk. 2:22-24).*

This passage repeats exactly the requirements of the Law in Leviticus, 12:8:

> *Such is the law concerning a woman who gives birth to either a boy or a girl. If she cannot afford a lamb, she is to take two turtledoves or two young pigeons, one for the holocaust and the other for the sacrifice for sin. The priest is to perform the rite of atonement over her and she will be purified.*

We understand why Mary and Joseph offered two doves; although they were descendants of David they were too poor to offer a lamb.

The sacrifice offered by the parents had been preceded by the consecration of the child, that is, by his circumcision.

This practice goes back to Abraham:

> *God said to Abraham, "You on your part shall maintain my Covenant, yourself and your descendants after you, generation after generation. Now this is my Covenant which you are to maintain between myself and you, and your descendants*

after you: all your males must be circumcised. . . . My Cove-
nant shall be marked on your bodies as a Covenant in perpe-
tuity (Gn. 17:10-13).

Circumcision, like many other Jewish customs, was practiced originally among the pagans, or at least before the beginning of monotheism, and was first a social custom rather than
a religious one. It was a rite initiating into marriage and the
life of the clan. Beginning with Abraham it became a sign both
to God and to man reminding them of the covenant that
bound them together and its attendant obligations. This sign
is a little like the rainbow at the time of the covenant with
Noah, or like the special articles of clothing, *tsitsith* and *tallith*
which constantly remind the Jew of his special vocation.

Therefore, since the day when Abraham circumcised his son
Isaac, circumcision became vital to the tradition of Israel. As
the prophet Jeremiah intimated, the earth and heaven depend
upon the keeping of the covenant (cf. Jr. 31:35).

Except in extreme situations, such as the crossing of the
desert, circumcision was carried out on the eighth day after
birth.

It seems that when circumcision was first practiced on the
eighth day, the operation was performed by the mother her-
self. But by the time of Jesus this was no longer the case. A
specialist, called the *Mohel*, performed this rite in the presence
of the parents, and in the presumed presence of the prophet
Elijah, who in such circumstances fulfilled his role as the
herald of the coming of the Messiah. Later, as one form of ritual succeeded another, a chair was set out for the prophet Elijah
on which the child was laid before his operation by the *Mohel*.
Elijah, the precursor of the Messiah, presided over the circumcision in spirit, since any newborn child might be the Messiah.

Among the blessings which still sanctify this ceremony, some
date back to the period of the Second Temple, and were
therefore in use at the time of Jesus. The surgical rite is now

preceded by: "Blessed art thou, O Lord our God, King of the universe, who hast hallowed us by thy commandments, and hast given us command concerning the Circumcision" (*ADPB*, p. 1027).

When the operation is over, the father recites another blessing: "Blessed art thou, O Lord our God, King of the universe, who hast hallowed us by thy commandments, and hast commanded us to make our sons enter into the covenant of Abraham our father" (*Ibid.*).

And the people attending the ceremony answer: "Even as this child has entered into the covenant, so may he enter into the Torah, the nuptial canopy, and into good deeds" (*Ibid.*).

Such is the Jewish rite described in Luke 2:21: "When the eighth day came and the child was to be circumcised . . . ." Joseph gave the newborn child the name *Yeshua*, which became Jesus.

The wound was treated with cumin powder and a certain bog myrtle which was pulverized for that purpose, and then, as tradition prescribed, with an ointment of oil and wine. The dressing, wrapped in fine linen and fastened with a red string, was to remain eight days. Twenty-five days more, that is to say, until the fortieth day after Jesus' birth, Mary observed the Law as Moses transmitted it: ". . . and she must wait another thirty-three days for her blood to be purified" (Lv. 12:4).

On the appointed day Mary and Joseph went up to the Temple, Mary carrying the child Jesus in her arms. She entered through the Door of the Newly Born on the east side, to the left of the Door of Nicanor. Joseph held the two doves which he had bought from a dealer on the Mount of Olives and gave the doves to a priest.

From the women's gallery Mary saw the priest cut the throat of one of the doves and burn the bird on the altar. Henceforth she could consider her son as belonging to the Covenant and ready to take his place in the sacred universe of the Jewish world of prayer.

For Jesus, as for any Jew 2,000 years ago, every moment of

his existence, every one of his actions, was steeped in the
sacred, in the invisible and the immaterial, and this affected
his whole destiny. The Gospels witness to the constant presence of the Spirit surrounding Jesus and to the constant impact
of prayer on him. They do so in the style of thought that is
theirs. Sometimes it coincides with Jewish spirituality and at
other times it is distinct from it. Yet, on the essential fact of the
omnipresence and the power of the Spirit the two traditions
meet, even though they may differ on the texts or the thrust
and purpose of prayer.

In the Gospels this view of the universe is very often seen in
the blessings which Jesus uses in the course of his preaching.
He follows, for instance, the Jewish rites which he knew as a
child. The purpose of these blessings is to make every product
of the soil sacred. In the Gospels on a number of different occasions he blessed bread and other food, such as fish.

> He gave orders that the people were to sit down on the
> grass; then he took the five loaves and the two fish, raised his
> eyes to heaven and said the blessing. And breaking the loaves
> he handed them to his disciples who gave them to the crowds
> (Mt. 14:19).

> . . . and he took the seven loaves and the fish, and he gave
> thanks and broke them and handed them to the disciples who
> gave them to the crowds (Mt. 15:36).

> Now as they were eating, Jesus took some bread, and when
> he had said the blessing he broke it and gave it to the disciples.
> "Take it and eat it"; he said "this is my body" (Mt. 26:26).

All these blessings over bread, food and wine reproduce almost exactly the original Jewish liturgy which Jesus knew during his childhood and his religious formation at Nazareth.
One finds two aspects in the synagogue and home rituals: the
personal and the corporate. On the one hand, there is the recognition by each believer of the sacred nature of the universe

which he confirms and strengthens throughout his life by his obedience to the Law. On the other hand, he comes to understand that these blessings are not isolated acts accomplished by one man; they are shared by a group of the faithful in whose name the celebrant pronounces the words of consecration. Therefore, the blessing comes from the whole group attending the liturgy. It is not one man praying for himself, as is too often the case in modern liturgies.

Rather than making petitions, the characteristic Jewish prayer of that day brought to God the commitment of entire communities. When man prays, he increases the total religious potential of the universe without knowing, naturally, whether he himself will benefit directly. But he knows that the community to which he belongs and the age in which he lives will be improved, purified and sanctified. This is close to the concept firmly established in Jewish tradition that each is responsible for his acts and benefits from them, not so much in relation to himself as in relation to the cosmic order, which he does have the power to alter for better or for worse. Jewish prayer, then, consists in reinforcing God's action in the universe rather than in modifying it according to personal needs—a more recent view of prayer. It does not ask for miraculous intervention which goes beyond natural laws: the permanent miracles of life and of the universe are sufficient.

One must understand that in such a setting, steeped in religion, the act of blessing is, for Jesus as for any Jew of his time, the key to his relationship with the universe. All events of daily life or natural phenomena are greeted with an appropriate blessing. And this network of blessings is, for each Jew and the whole of Israel, the basis of their participation in the life of the universe and in the unfolding of history.

Even modern Jews are linked with a tradition thousands of years old when they practice the religion of their ancestors. For example, the writer recalls an occasion when he was attending the Rabbinical School in Paris. Lightning and thunder interrupted the class. The professor rose from his chair, went to the window and said the appropriate blessing: "Blessed art thou, O Lord our God, King of the universe, whose strength and power fill the world."

By acknowledging thunder with a blessing, the rabbi accepted nature with all its hostility to man and submitted to it as do the rest of God's creatures, whether they be animal, plant or mineral. But even more important, through this act proper only to men he was strengthening the sacred nature of the world and filling it with the divine. Moreover, a man of the twentieth century was continuing a tradition which goes back almost to the origins of time.

The words, *Baruch Adonai*, "Blessed be the Lord," the most ancient and holy of blessings, were already in use at the time of the patriarchs, the judges and the kings. They can be found in Genesis (24:27):

> "... *Blessed be Yahweh, God of my master Abraham, for he has not stopped showing kindness and goodness to my master. Yahweh has guided my steps to the house of my master's brother,*" *Eliezer says as he meets Rebekah at the spring.*

In Exodus 18:10-11, we find the blessing used by Jethro, Moses' father-in-law, who was then a priest of Midian and who was to become the first proselyte, that is, the first non-Jew to observe the commandments of the Law.

> ... "*Blessed be Yahweh,*" *said Jethro then* "*who has rescued you from the Egyptians and from Pharaoh, and has rescued the people from the grasp of the Egyptians. Now I know that Yahweh is greater than all the gods. ...*"

The prayer appears in Ruth, Samuel and Kings, and also in the Psalms, for instance:

> *Blessed be Yahweh, for he hears*
> *the sound of my petition! (Ps. 28:6).*

> *Blessed be Yahweh, who performs*
> *marvels of love for me*
> *in a fortress-city! (Ps. 31:21).*

These blessings which constantly accompany Israel through all the vicissitudes of history are of divine origin. In the beginning, God alone blessed. Later, he allowed his creatures to share in this essential function.

Such manifestation of trust, a sharing of his divine attributes with those who accomplish his law on earth, we see in the story of Abraham. According to Rashi, a French rabbi of the eleventh century and one of the masters of rabbinical commentary, at the moment of Abraham's calling, of his departure for his priestly mission God gave him the power of blessing. "Yahweh said to Abram, "Leave your country, your family and your father's house, for the land I will show you" (Gn. 12:1).

Commenting on the following verse: "I will bless you and make your name so famous that it will be used as a blessing," Rashi leaves no doubt: "You will be entrusted with the power of blessing."

So from now on Abraham is entitled to bless. In such a way does God provide man with the freedom and the consecration to play a role in creation both concrete and exalted.

In the context of this important role, the details of praying matter little. "How does one pray?" the Talmud asks. That seems unimportant. It is said that one of the disciples of Eliezer used to pray at great length. Others of his disciples exclaimed: "Master, how long he prays!"

"Does he pray longer," replied Eliezer, "than Moses our master, of whom it is written that *he prayed forty days and forty nights?*" (Dt. 9:25).

Another disciple, however, was shortening his prayer. "Master, what a brief prayer!" said the others.

"Is it shorter than that of our master Moses? For it is written: Moses cried to Yahweh, 'O God,' he said, 'please heal her, I beg you' " (Nb. 12:13).

Clearly, therefore, the essential thing is to pray and to bless. We read in the Talmud: "It is written: 'To Yahweh belongs earth and all it holds, the world and all who live in it' " (Ps. 24:1). Consequently whoever enjoys anything in the world without first saying a prayer commits theft. To prevent such illegitimate and profane use of God's world, it is therefore imperative that Jews continue to participate through blessing in the world's worship of its Lord.

Let us give some examples. When one sees strangely formed persons such as giants or dwarfs, one says : "Blessed art thou, O Lord our God, King of the universe, who dost diversify the forms of thy creatures." When one meets a sick man, or a cripple or a wretched creature, the blessing must counteract this physical injustice: "Blessed be the just Judge" (Talmud of Jerusalem).

In addition to these exceptional cases, there are blessings which fit more usual circumstances and actions. Here are a few of the one hundred blessings which punctuate the day of a Jew and that of the young Jesus.

According to the commentaries on Numbers (Nb. *rabba* 18), this collection of one hundred blessings was gathered by King David and was certainly in use at the time of Jesus' birth. Those which are said daily accompany the Jew throughout his day from night to morning, and from morning to night. They marked out the hours of Jesus' childhood. Through them we can visualize his day as it unfolded in Nazareth. Before retiring for the night, he would in his parents' presence say some such prayer as:

> *Blessed art thou, O Lord our God, King of the universe, who makest the bands of sleep to fall upon mine eyes, and slumber upon mine eyelids. May it be thy will, O Lord my God, and God of my fathers, to suffer me to lie down in peace and to let me rise up again in peace. Let not my thoughts trouble me, nor evil dreams, nor evil fancies, but let my rest be perfect before thee. O lighten mine eyes, lest I sleep the sleep of death, for it is thou who givest light to the apple of the eye.*

*Blessed art thou, O Lord, who givest light to the whole world
in thy glory* (ADPB, *p. 997*; cf. *Ps. 13:4; 17:8*).

Sleep, according to the Talmud, has an affinity with death:
"Sleep is the sixtieth part of death," just as the Sabbath is the
sixtieth part of the delights of the next life. It is understanda-
ble, therefore, that at the moment of awakening when the soul
returns to the body, blessings should be said to evoke the idea
of resurrection. Some rabbis recommend the formula: "Blessed
art thou, O Lord our God, King of the universe, who givest life
to the dead." Others develop the same idea in verses of great
intensity:

> *O my God, the soul which thou gavest me is pure. Thou didst
> create it, thou didst form it, thou didst breathe it into me.
> Thou preservest it within me, but wilt restore it unto me
> hereafter. So long as the soul is within me, I will give thanks
> unto thee, O Lord my God—God of my fathers, Sovereign of
> all works, Lord of all souls. Blessed art thou, O Lord, who re-
> storest souls unto the dead* (Ibid., *p. 19*).

Upon awakening, Jesus certainly blessed God again for having restored him to consciousness, thought and action. His
first gestures as he emerges from sleep, are accompanied by
blessings. As he opens his eyes he says: "Blessed art thou, O
Lord our God, King of the universe, who openest the eyes of
the blind" (*Ibid.*, p. 21). As he rises and stretches he says:
"Blessed art thou, O Lord our God, King of the universe, who
settest free them that are bound" (*Ibid.*, p. 23).

Naturally, from that moment on his washing and dressing
will also be preceded by blessings. When washing his hands
he says: "Blessed art thou, O Lord our God, King of the universe, who hast hallowed us by thy commandments, and given
us command concerning the washing of the hands" (*Ibid.*, p. 9).

Then he blesses the normal functions of the body by saying:
"Blessed art thou, O Lord our God, King of the universe, who
hast formed man in wisdom, and created in him many pas-

sages and vessels. . . . Blessed art thou, O Lord, who art the wondrous healer of all flesh" (Ibid., p. 11).

Before he dresses, he says another blessing which is both precise and general: "Blessed art thou, O Lord our God, King of the universe, who clothest the naked" (Ibid., p. 23).

When he rises: "Blessed art thou, O Lord our God, King of the universe, who raisest up them that are bowed down" (Ibid.).

When he is standing: "Blessed art thou, O Lord our God, King of the universe, who spreadest forth the earth above the waters" (Ibid.).

At the first steps he takes: "Blessed art thou, O Lord our God, King of the universe, who hast made firm the steps of man" (Ibid.).

When he puts on his sandals: "Blessed art thou, O Lord our God, King of the universe, who providest my every want" (Ibid.).

As he puts on his belt: "Blessed art thou, O Lord our God, King of the universe, who girdest Israel with might" (Ibid.).

As he puts on his head-dress: "Blessed art thou, O Lord our God, King of the universe, who crownest Israel with glory" (Ibid.).

Four other blessings must also be said each morning by the young Jesus. They are related to being a Jewish male:

Blessed art thou, O Lord, who bestowest loving
kindnesses upon thy people Israel (Ibid, p. 25).

Blessed art thou, O Lord our God, King of the
universe, who hast not made me a heathen (Ibid.,
p. 19).

Blessed art thou, O Lord our God, King of the
universe, who hast not made me a woman (Ibid.,
p. 21).

Blessed art thou, O Lord our God, King of the
universe, who hast not made me a bondman (Ibid.).

Finally, there is a blessing belonging both to everyday life and to the liturgy, a blessing supposedly inspired by angels which Jesus repeats either as he rises or as he falls asleep. It is the basic prayer of the *Shema*:

> *Thou wast the same ere the world was created; thou hast been the same since the world hath been created; thou art the same in this world, and thou wilt be the same in the world to come. . . . . Sanctify thy Name throughout thy world. . .* (Ibid., p. 31).

Still more blessings are recited at meals:

Blessing over the bread: "Blessed art thou, O Lord our God, King of the universe, who bringest forth bread from the earth" (*Ibid.*, p. 963).

Over the wine: "Blessed art thou, O Lord our God, King of the universe, who createst the fruit of the vine" (*Ibid.*, p. 985).

Over the food: "Blessed art thou, O Lord our God, King of the universe, who createst various kinds of food" (*Ibid.*).

Over the fruit of the trees: "Blessed art thou, O Lord our God, King of the universe, for the tree and the fruit of the tree" (*Ibid.*).

Over the products of the soil: "Blessed art thou, O Lord our God, King of the universe, for the produce of the field" (*Ibid.*).

Then the blessing when the meal is over: "Blessed art thou, O Lord our God, King of the universe, who givest food unto all" (*Ibid.*, p. 981).

If the food is not the product of the soil: "Blessed art thou, O Lord our God, King of the universe, by whose word all things exist" (*Ibid.*, p. 989).

There are other blessings for gifts other than food, for instance, for a sweet scent:

> *Blessed art thou, O Lord our God, King of the*
> *universe, who createst fragrant woods,*
> > *who createst fragrant plants,*
> > *who givest a goodly scent to fruits,*
> > *who createst diverse kinds of spices,*
> > *who createst fragrant oils* (Ibid., pp. 989-991).

When one sees the buds of spring:

> *Blessed art thou, O Lord our God, King of the universe, who*
> *hast made thy world lacking in nought, but hast produced*
> *therein goodly creatures and goodly trees wherewith to give*
> *delight unto the children of men* (Ibid., p. 991).

When one receives good news: "Blessed art thou, O Lord our God, King of the universe, who art good and dispensest good" (*Ibid.*, p. 993).

When one meets a friend after a year's separation or when one rises from an illness: "Blessed art thou, O Lord our God, King of the universe, who bringest back the dead to life. Blessed be the merciful who brought us back to him and not to death."

Some blessings are meant to resist idolatry. When coming to a place where it was formerly practiced: "Blessed art thou, O Lord our God, King of the universe, who hast banished idolatry from this place."

But if idolatry is still practiced there: "Blessed art thou, O Lord our God, King of the universe, who hast been patient with those who disobey thy will."

When he puts a *mezuza* upon his door, that is to say, a tube made from wood or from a reed containing the words of the *Shema*, he blesses God who has sanctified us by his commandments and has ordered us to affix a *mezuza*. Thus there is no moment or circumstance in which Jesus, with all Jews, cannot contribute to the fulfillment of God's will in the world of his creation.

All these daily blessings of which we have been speaking, blessings over the humblest acts of life, are but an echo of another blessing, the most basic, the most profound in the ancient Jewish liturgy: the priestly blessing. It is this blessing which gives all the rest their true dimension. This priestly blessing is pronounced at each service of the synagogue or of the Temple by the officiating minister, rabbi, priest or member of the community, and is in fact the blessing of God himself. It is, therefore, the most moving moment of any Jewish liturgy. It is no longer men blessing the ordinary acts of their lives to reinforce the divine action; it is God himself blessing and sanctifying the children of Israel.

Clearly this form of blessing would speak to the divine aspect of the child Jesus, just as the daily blessings would address his humanity. Each contributes to the balance between the secular and the sacred which is essential to the religion of Israel.

Though men may sanctify every place and moment of the secular order, they do so only because God in his turn has given them the power of Abraham to bless. There is in this way a kind of Jacob's ladder between heaven and earth, between the Creator and his creatures. Prayers and blessings never go in one direction only. The priestly blessing which was invoked over the child Jesus, therefore, originated in the blessing pronounced by Aaron and his sons, according to the command of Numbers 6:22-27:

> The Lord said to Moses, "Say to Aaron and his sons,
> Thus you shall bless the people of Israel: you shall say to them,
> The Lord bless you and keep you:
> The Lord make his face to shine upon you, and be gracious to you:
> The Lord lift up his countenance upon you, and give you peace.
> So shall they put my name upon the people of Israel, and I will bless them" (RSV.).

We find such a priestly blessing in several places in the Pentateuch: once at the time of Aaron's investiture as high priest (Lv. 9:22), and on many other occasions as the function of the so-called Levitical priesthood (Dt. 10:8; 21:5; Jos. 8:33; 2 Ch. 30:37).

The priestly blessing was accompanied by gestures that emphasized its sanctity. In the Temple at Jerusalem the priests raised their hands as high as their heads. In other places those who gave the blessing raised their hands only to the level of their shoulders. In the Temple during the blessing the priests spoke only the letters of the sacred *Tetragram*, Y-H-W-H, that being the only possible way of uttering the name of God. Elsewhere, an equivalent, almost a circumlocution, was used: *Adonai*, "the Lord." In the Temple the people answered: "Blessed be the Lord, the God of Israel, for ever and ever." In other places, however, the people's response was simply *Amen*. There was, therefore, a clear distinction between a service in the Temple and a service celebrated elsewhere, for instance, in the synagogue. But later, after the death of Simon the Just (circa 300 B.C.), the *Tetragram* was no longer pronounced publicly even in the Temple, so that no unworthy or irreverent person could profane the sacred name.

Either by using the letters Y-H-W-H, or the equivalent, *Adonai*, the fundamental idea behind the priest's blessing was to "imprint" the name of God upon the children of Israel.

The sacredness connected with the name of God gave to such acts of blessing an almost mystical quality. Hence the belief that while the priest raised his hands, the *Shekinah* — the presence of God — hovered above the faithful, its rays passing through the fingers of the priest at that moment. The people were not allowed to watch, lest they be struck with blindness or other adversity such as those who looked upon the Ark in ancient times had suffered.

In the Temple the blessing was announced in the following words: "Our God and God of our Fathers, bless us, thy holy people, with the threefold blessing of the Torah, written by thy servant Moses, spoken by Aaron and his sons."

Then the priest stood over the congregation and offered this silent prayer:

Let it be thy will, O Lord our God, that this blessing with

*which you have commanded us to bless thy people Israel, may
be a perfect blessing; let it be granted with neither fault nor
lack, now and for ever.*

It is important to observe, however, that the priest does not
act as a mediator in such a ceremony, for the very notion of
mediator is unknown in Israel. It is not the priest, strictly
speaking, who blesses. It is God who affirms through him: *"I
will bless them."*

It is in this way that the young Jesus was blessed. One can
imagine the special meaning which these priestly words from
God took on for him as his sense of vocation became clearer.

On the eve of his departure for Jerusalem at the threshold of
adolescence and consecration, Jesus was fully aware that the
most insignificant of his acts of devotion was actually a con-
tribution to and a confirmation of the action of the Lord, by
which his ineffable and ever-present name was inscribed on
the destiny of every child of Israel.

2. In the Shadow of the Synagogue

THERE ARE MANY REFERENCES in the Gospels to the presence of Christ in the synagogue and to his participation in the services. Nine texts, three from Matthew, three from Mark, two from Luke and one from John mention in almost identical terms the occasions on which Jesus taught in the synagogues.

> He went round the whole of Galilee teaching in their synagogues, proclaiming the Good News of the kingdom and curing all kinds of diseases and sickness among the people (Mt. 4:23).

> Jesus made a tour through all the towns and villages, teaching in their synagogues, proclaiming the Good News of the kingdom and curing all kinds of diseases and sickness (Mt. 9:35).

> . . . and, coming to his home town, he taught the people in their synagogue in such a way that they were astonished and

said, "Where did the man get this wisdom and these miraculous powers?" (Mt. 13:54).

They went as far as Capernaum, and as soon as the sabbath came he went to the synagogue and began to teach. And his teaching made a deep impression on them because, unlike the scribes, he taught them with authority (Mk. 1:21-22).

And he went all through Galilee, preaching in their synagogues and casting out devils (Mk. 1:39).

Going from that district, he went to his home town and his disciples accompanied him. With the coming of the sabbath he began teaching in the synagogue and most of them were astonished when they heard him. They said, "Where did the man get all this? What is this wisdom that has been granted him, and these miracles that are worked through him?" (Lk. 6:1-2).

Jesus, with the power of the Spirit in him, returned to Galilee; and his reputation spread throughout the countryside. He taught in their synagogues and everyone praised him (Lk. 4:14-15).

He taught this doctrine at Capernaum, in the synagogue (Jn. 6:59).

And he continued preaching in the synagogues of Judaea (Lk. 4:44).

The purpose of the synagogue service was twofold: to pray and to offer the ritual blessings, and to instruct the faithful on the content and meaning of the Law and the Prophets. Readings from these were included in the Saturday morning service. Five times in the Gospel according to Matthew, Jesus quotes passages from the Decalogue:

You have learnt how it was said to our ancestors: You must not kill; and if anyone does kill he must answer for it before the court (Mt. 5:21).

You have learnt how it was said: You must not commit adultery *(Mt. 5:27).*

Again, you have learnt how it was said to our ancestors: You must not break your oath, but must fulfil your oaths to the Lord *(Mt. 5:33).*

For God said: Do your duty to your father and mother and: Anyone who curses father or mother must be put to death *(Mt. 15:4).*

Jesus said to him, "Why do you ask me about what is good? There is one alone who is good. But if you wish to enter into life, keep the commandments." He said, "Which?" "These": Jesus replied *"*You must not kill. You must not commit adultery. You must not bring false witness. Honour your father and mother, *and*: You must love your neighbour as yourself*" (Mt. 19:17-19).*

Other passages in the Gospels allude to the other aspect of the synagogue service.

On one occasion, described by Matthew, Mark and Luke, Jesus quotes one of the basic prayers of Israel which always marks a climactic moment in the service, the *Shema.* As we shall see later, it includes a proclamation of the oneness of God and directions on how to honor him.

One of the scribes who had listened to them debating and had observed how well Jesus had answered them, now came up and put a question to him, "Which is the first of all the commandments?" Jesus replied, "This is the first: Listen, Israel, the Lord our God is the one Lord, and you must love the Lord your God with all your heart, with all your soul, with all your mind and with all your strength*" (Mk. 12:28-30; cf. Mt. 22:36-40; Lk. 10:25-28).*

This reference to portions of the liturgy of the synagogue brings to mind two other important passages. One is a text in Matthew in which Jesus affirms his commitment to the Law.

> *Do not imagine that I have come to abolish the Law or the Prophets. I have come not to abolish but to complete them. I tell you solemnly, till heaven and earth disappear, not one dot, not one little stroke, shall disappear from the Law until its purpose is achieved. Therefore, the man who infringes even one of the least of these commandments and teaches others to do the same will be considered the least in the kingdom of heaven; but the man who keeps them and teaches them will be considered great in the kingdom of heaven (Mt. 5:17-19).*

The other texts are found in Isaiah and Luke where we see Jesus taking part in a Sabbath service at Nazareth. Here again Jesus is teaching, and it is evident that he observed a ritual still in use today:

> *He came to Nazara, where he had been brought up, and went into the synagogue on the sabbath day as he usually did. He stood up to read, and they handed him the scroll of the prophet Isaiah. Unrolling the scroll he found the place where it is written:*

> > *"The spirit of the Lord has been given to me,*
> > *for Yahweh has anointed me.*
> > *He has sent me to bring good news to the poor,*
> > *to bind up hearts that are broken;*
> > *to proclaim liberty to captives,*
> > *freedom to those in prison;*
> > *to proclaim a year of favour from Yahweh, . . ."*

> *He then rolled up the scroll, gave it back to the assistant and sat down. And all eyes in the synagogue were fixed upon him (Lk. 4:16-20; Is. 61:1-2).*

All these passages from the Gospels leave no doubt that Jesus prayed and taught in various synagogues, and especially in that of his own village, Nazareth.

In Nazareth, in an enclosed field belonging to the cathedral, one can still see buried in the ground a crypt which is said to have been the synagogue of the village two thousand years ago. It is small and might have held a hundred people at most—a very simple place, appropriate to a province well known for its rustic ways. Moreover, the synagogue is not the Temple; the synagogue is not a consecrated sanctuary. It is a meeting place, a kind of parish hall where a service can be held with as few as ten men present. Professional clergy are not attached to such a place. The rabbi, if there be one, is not a priest, or, rather, he is no more priest that all the other children of Israel, who, since Sinai, are all priests. It is simply that the rabbi is distinguished from these lay priests because he has studied more extensively and has a better knowledge of the Bible and tradition. He may love God with more awareness and fidelity; he may put into better practice the commandments of the Torah and especially the basic law of love formulated in Leviticus 19:18, "You must love your neighbor as yourself." But all of this which may invest him with a special authority among the assembly of "priests," and perhaps makes of him a kind of lay superior in the village community, confers on him no special privilege. At most he has greater competence in celebrating religious ceremonies. Any Jew marked in his flesh with the sign of the Covenant and having attained at the age of thirteen his religious maturity, called *Bar Mitzvah*, may officiate. In Nazareth, in any Jewish assembly of the time, and today in many synagogues or houses of study, one or another of the faithful officiates in turn.

Let us suppose we are now in the synagogue of Nazareth about an hour before sundown on a Friday in one of the early years of the Christian era, that is to say, around the year 3975 of the creation of world, 3975 of the Jewish era. It is early in the month of *Nisan* the Friday preceding the journey to Jerusalem where, according to Luke, Jesus is going to celebrate Passover. He is in his thirteenth year, and for the first time he will accompany his family in anticipation of his religious initiation which will take place on his return from the Holy City.

It is almost twilight. When the first star appears in the sky the Sabbath will begin. For twenty-four hours, until the first star appears the following day, secular life will cease in the Jewish community of Nazareth, as in all other Jewish communities in the world, where is professed the worship of the One God: Hear, O Israel: the Lord Is Our God, the Lord Is One (the *Shema*) and the law of love: *Thou shalt love thy neighbor as thyself.*

An hour will elapse between the beginning of the Sabbath and the time when the faithful will pass through the door of the synagogue. During this short interval between secular and sacred time, what do the inhabitants of Nazareth do, what does Jesus' family do? The women finish the household chores which will be forbidden to them during twenty-four hours. They finish cooking food for the three meals that will follow, since they will not be allowed to make a fire during the holy day. They light the lamps which will burn continuously until dawn, since they will not be allowed to touch them for twenty-four hours. Perhaps Mary, daughter of Joachim, draws water at the Fountain of the Virgin at the edge of the old city.

Men purify themselves of all the blemishes of the week in a ritual bath. They don their festive attire and prepare their prayer shawls trimmed with tassels, which will be put on the following day.

In this interval between sacred and secular time each male adult in Israel prepares to visibly assume the priesthood which since Sinai has been his responsibility in the world, among the "nations"—the *goyim*—those who share the Covenant of the Rainbow but not the Covenant of Sinai.

The synagogue of Nazareth will soon be filled with the faithful. As twilight deepens the vault is lighted only by the last rays of the setting sun and by the flickering of an oil lamp which throughout the day symbolizes the divine spirit abiding in the place where men will gather.

In spite of the growing darkness, two silhouettes stand out on the *tebah*, the very simple and rudimentary platform where the celebrant will soon recite prayers and read the Law and the Prophets. They can be seen directly in front of the lectern where, during the Saturday morning service, the scrolls of the Torah and of the Prophets will be displayed with great solemnity.

One is an adult, the other a child of twelve, his limbs still slender, his voice still high. He repeats in a treble voice some ritual chants intoned by the adult who seems to be his teacher submitting him to a kind of test.

The service will begin in an hour.

The tabernacle, which is at the back of the room behind the *tebah*, the *aron-ha-kodesh*, is open. The scroll of the Law, the *Sefer Torah*, is usually laid there. It has just been taken out and rests on the lectern.

The teacher, using a pointer, guides the child in reading the inspired lines written on the scroll. The boy frames his chanting of the Sabbatical lessons with ritual blessings, and practices reading the Law as if the synagogue were full, as if the ten persons required for the celebration of the worship had already gathered and the service had begun.

This is a kind of rehearsal. The adult finds out whether his pupil will be able to read the *Parashah* in public at the time of his profession of faith. Almost every Friday the same procedure is repeated for a child who is preparing himself to share in the greatness and the fate of Israel. His voice may tremble with emotion as he tries to reproduce faithfully the intonations and gestures of his teacher, who may be the rabbi or the synagogue cantor. The latter is probably an artisan of Nazareth whose deep voice is suited to the sacred words written on the *Sefer Torah*. In this particular case the teacher may even be Joseph, the father of the neophyte, Jesus.

The lesson is over, the scrolls of the Law are rolled up and put back in the tabernacle, which remains closed during the Friday evening service. Jesus and his teacher leave the synagogue to join their families in their preparations for the service.

On the threshold of his thirteenth year, on the eve of his trip to Jerusalem where the doctors of the Temple will evaluate his knowledge of religion and of Hebrew (the sacred language of a people who usually speak Aramaic) Jesus prepares himself to take part in the service of the synagogue. Leaving childhood, he is preparing to prove whether he is capable of officiating and praying in public.

The Friday evening service, which Jesus and Joseph attend with their neighbors, does not include, as does the Saturday morning service, the reading of the Law and the Prophets; it is composed of blessings and prayers which for about an hour introduce the faithful into the sacred world of the Sabbath.

Ma tovou . . . these are the first words that Jesus hears and very likely repeats before entering the house of prayer.

> *How goodly are thy tents, O Jacob, thy dwelling place, O Israel! As for me, in the abundance of thy loving kindness will I come into thy house: I will worship toward thy holy temple in the fear of thee. Lord, I love the habitation of thy house, and the place where thy glory dwelleth. I will worship and bow down: I will bend the knee before the Lord, my Maker. May my prayer unto thee, O Lord, be in an acceptable time: O God, in the abundance of thy loving kindness, answer me with thy sure salvation* (ADPB, p. 5).

Then the young Jesus watches Joseph raise his hand and hears his comment on this gesture: "When I raise my hands towards thy sanctuary, O Lord my God, I pray to thee and thou hearest."

So ends the brief walk taking him from home to the center of the synagogue, that is, from the dwelling place of men to the place where they meet with God. They walk to the accompaniment of ritual prayer. Although this walk through familiar streets is no different from other walks, it has become a spiritual ascent, and Jesus begins to sense the simplicity as well as the sublimity of the religion of Israel. He may even remember a precept of his time subsequently recorded in the Talmud:

"Always follow the paths of the earth." To go to the synagogue, Jesus followed those paths.

After the first prayer at the threshold, Jesus and Joseph proceed to the place reserved for men, while Mary, his mother, sits at the back on one of the benches reserved for women. Perhaps during the service, her son turns and exchanges with his mother glances full of love and fervor.

Then comes a psalm appropriate to the arrival of the congregation. It is a Davidic song of ascent recalling, in this humble village crypt, the emotion and pride inspired by the majestic sight of the Temple at Jerusalem.

> How I rejoiced when they said to me,
>   "Let us go to the house of Yahweh!"
> And now our feet are standing
>   in your gateways, Jerusalem.
>
> Jerusalem restored! The city,
>   one united whole!
> Here the tribes come up,
>   the tribes of Yahweh,
>
> they come to praise Yahweh's name,
>   as he ordered Israel,
> here where the tribunals of justice are,
>   the royal tribunals of David.
>
> Pray for peace in Jerusalem,
>   "Prosperity to your houses!"
> Peace inside your city walls!
>   Prosperity to your palaces!"
>
> Since all are my brothers and friends,
>   I say "Peace be with you!"
> Since Yahweh our God lives here,
>   I pray for your happiness (Ps. 122).

Only then does the service begin.

Jesus has already taken his place in the house of prayer. He now comes into the timeless realm of prayer. It is a crucial moment and deserves our attention.

A Jew may worship in any place whatsoever provided there be ten men present, the number required to utter the blessings glorifying God, *Barekhu, Kedusha, Kaddish*. This quorum is called the *minian*. He may worship under a roof or in the open, in a private house or in an assembly hall. His prayers are always valid and effective.

Although he is allowed to conduct this divine service at any point in space, he may do it only at certain appointed times. This is because the religion of Israel, the religion of Jesus, is the first in which God writes his name on the unfolding scrolls of history and of time. It is the first in which time and history are God's time and history. Therefore, this religion builds its monuments only rarely in space. Pagan religions or religions rivalling them in pomp and ceremonial may build monuments dedicated to their cults: the ziggurats, the towers of Babel or the temples of Jupiter, whose strength and grandeur are necessary to witness to the glory of ephemeral gods. The people of Israel, too, were allowed to celebrate their cult in a temple, but the place of worship had so little ultimate importance that even the Temple was allowed by God to be destroyed. The people of Israel took the commandments of God into the desert with them. They set down the Ark of the Covenant wherever they were, and surrounded it with a pattern of daily prayer which created the only sanctuary that could not be destroyed or captured.

Of course, the Jews also have their monuments. Judaism has its sanctuaries, but the fact remains that these are not in space but in time. The Jews are the "builders of time" (Heschel), who, each Sabbath, each Holy Day, recharge with spirituality the emptiness of the moments which otherwise would be lost in the dull, automatic succession of days and minutes. The Sabbath, which Jesus took part in physically and spiritually, is, according to the Law and tradition, the moment when God interrupted his work to contemplate his creation, the moment when man, the Jew, is allowed to suspend his work for one day to devote himself to God.

According to the Law, the seventh day is God's day of rest:

> *Thus heaven and earth were completed with all their array. On the seventh day God completed the work he had been doing. He rested on the seventh day after all the work he had been doing. God blessed the seventh day and made it holy, because on that day he had rested after all his work of creating (Gn. 2:1-3).*

It is also the day in which God commanded men to rest. Even in the desert, to sustain the life of the Hebrews there, God sent a ration of manna every day sufficient for their needs; they were to eat it immediately. By the following day it would spoil. But on the sixth day a double ration of manna fell from the heavens, and that manna was such that it did not spoil. Through the wonder of this miracle which, like all Jewish miracles, fits into the natural course of events, God wanted to tell his people that the seventh day, being freed from practical problems, could be devoted entirely to prayer. This is the origin of the Sabbath.

So on that day even the desert, empty of dwellings and monuments, resounded also with prayers and blessings which for Israel constitute the only true and enduring sanctuary.

So it is that in the winding alleys of Nazareth and in the streets of the ghettos which were later to enclose the people of God, houses fill with prayer and ring with melody older and more lasting than their walls. The true monument of Israel is not made of stones but of the songs within them.

Therefore, it is this invisible but not unreal sanctuary that the young Jesus enters, this immaterial sanctuary of which the stone edifice is, by a strange paradox, only the reflection.

The pillars of this worship are the prayers bringing together the truths of the religion of Israel which are also the realities of the human condition: adoration of the Creator, knowledge of his Law and the vocation of Israel as the representative of the whole human race. These three truths find their way into time and history, without the necessity of being changed or charged with mystery.

At Jerusalem, on the other hand, Jesus will become familiar with a building in which strange mysteries take place: the high priest will shut himself in the secret recesses of the sanctuary to celebrate once a year, at *Yom Kippur*, the greatest mystery that exists: the utterance of the name of the Lord. Sacrifices and ceremonies such as that of the scapegoat will seek to interpret the only true offering, the only real expiation—that which takes place within the heart.

Although Jesus knew that the Temple of Jerusalem would soon be destroyed in accordance with the designs of Providence which first permitted its erection, this Temple of prayer which Jesus enters on the Sabbath symbolized the permanence of a people of family lines. It is eternal because it is founded on the constant succession of fleeting destinies which make up the ages of man, the eternity of Israel. It is not subject to time since it is time itself in its constant flow. In spite of all its trials, it remains indestructible. As long as days are days, Israel will be alive, chanting the same prayers, bowing at the same time in the liturgy which has remained essentially as it was at the time of Jesus. And not an "iota" of the Law can be erased.

The liturgy begins with prayer. In our modern synagogues after two thousand years, we can still hear in essence the same prayers which Jesus heard and said in his village of Nazareth. Some details may be different, but the inspiration is the same.

The Friday evening service may have begun then as it does now with Psalm 92, a song for the Sabbath:

> *It is good to give thanks to Yahweh,*
>   *to play in honour of your name, Most High,*
>   *to proclaim your love at daybreak*
>   *and your faithfulness all through the night*
>   *to the music of the zither and lyre,*
>   *to the rippling of the harp.*

I am happy, Yahweh, at what you have done;
at your achievements I joyfully exclaim,
"Great are your achievements, Yahweh,
immensely deep your thoughts!"
Stupid men are not aware of this,
fools can never appreciate it.

The wicked may sprout as thick as weeds
and every evil-doer flourish,
but only to be everlastingly destroyed,
whereas you are supreme for ever.
See how your enemies perish,
how all evil men are routed.

You raise my horn as if I were a wild ox,
you pour fresh oil on my head;
I was able to see those who were spying on me,
to overhear what the wicked were whispering,
so the virtuous flourish like palm trees
and grow as tall as the cedars of Lebanon.

Planted in the house of Yahweh,
they will flourish in the courts of our God,
still bearing fruit in old age,
still remaining fresh and green,
to proclaim that the Lord is righteous,
my rock in whom no fault is to be found!

Then followed the *Barekhu*, a solemn blessing which is still today a climax in the service. In sentences alternating between the leader and the congregation, characteristic of the Jewish liturgy and taken over by Christian worship—the responses pass from the tribune to the congregation, from the *tebah* to the *kehila*.

"Bless ye the Lord, who is to be blessed," proclaims the leader, turned towards the tabernacle (*ADPB*, p. 305).

And the whole congregation, standing, bows in the direction of the receptacle in which are laid the scrolls of the Law and answer as one voice:

"Blessed be the Lord, who is to be blessed forever and ever" (*Ibid.*). This must have been spoken with the intensity of the Jewish fervor which had encountered so many trials, been illuminated by so many hopes, soiled by so many faults and repudiations, exalted by so many piercing insights into the universe and God. It had inspired men of outstanding destiny. That prayer filled the vaults of the synagogue far better than could the swell of organs, or the *bel canto* flights of music which today so often misrepresent and parody prayer.

This blessing, both complete and terse, unites one to another and lifts the heart. Thus does the young Jesus come to share in the respectful intimacy unique to the relationship of the Jew with his Creator. The Lord is now present because the faithful have brought to remembrance his presence in the world and in history. Their prayers now unfold in an atmosphere both heavenly and human.

Then comes the reading of the Decalogue, the ten basic verses given by God at Sinai (Exodus 20). At the last service celebrated in the synagogue before the Paschal trip to Jerusalem these would seem especially relevant to Jesus, for the following week he and his family will be in the Temple to commemorate the Passover, the deliverance of Israel from Egypt in order that the chosen people might be at Sinai when God, through Moses' voice, would promulgate his Law and declare the ten fundamental words.

Ten verses: the first, the affirmation of God's existence; the second, third and fourth, religious precepts; and the six others, precepts of current morality to be obeyed by believers and unbelievers alike, by pagans and Jews. The whole is a blueprint, both religious and secular, for human life in the future. Such are the ten verses that Jesus hears proclaimed at the opening of the last Sabbath service he will attend in the synagogue of Nazareth and which on the eve of Passover take on special meaning.

> Anochi Adonai elohecha . . . *I am Yahweh your God who brought you out of the land of Egypt, out of the house of slavery.*

Lo Yihyé lecha . . . *You shall have no gods except me.*

You shall not make yourself a carved image or any likeness of anything in heaven or on earth beneath or in the waters under the earth; you shall not bow down to them or serve them. For I, Yahweh your God, am a jealous God and I punish the father's fault in the sons, the grandsons and the great-grandsons of those who hate me; but I show kindness to thousands of those who love me and keep my commandments.

Lo tissa eth schem Adonaï . . . *You shall not utter the name of Yahweh your God to misuse it, for Yahweh will not leave unpunished the man who utters his name to misuse it.*

Zachor et yom ha schabbat . . . *Remember the sabbath day and keep it holy. For six days you shall labour and do all your work, but the seventh day is a sabbath for Yahweh your God. You shall do no work that day, neither you nor your son nor your daughter nor your servants, men or women, nor your animals nor the stranger who lives with you. For in six days Yahweh made the heavens and the earth and the sea and all that these hold, but on the seventh day he rested; that is why Yahweh has blessed the sabbath day and made it sacred.*

Kabed ète avicha ve èth immécha . . . *Honour your father and your mother so that you may have a long life in the land that Yahweh your God has given to you.*

Lo tirtzah . . . *You shall not kill.*

Lo tineaf . . . *You shall not commit adultery.*

Lo tignov . . . *You shall not steal.*

Lo taané . . . *You shall not bear false witness against your neighbour.*

Lo toc'hmod . . . *You shall not covet your neighbour's house. You shall not covet your neighbour's wife, or his servant, man or woman, or his ox, or his donkey, or anything that is his* (Ex. 20:2-17).

These basic precepts, concise, simple and concrete, will nourish millennia of faith and survive centuries of unbelief and persecution, even though they will be temporarily omitted from the synagogue ritual during the seventy or eighty years following the time Jesus heard them at Nazareth. Unusual fervor still accompanies the reading of the Decalogue once a year. Among all the passages of the Bible read in the service, among all the *Parashoth*, this is the only one at which the faithful rise as they do at the time of the blessings and prayers. One can imagine the intensity and seriousness with which these words resounded under the simple roof of the house of prayer at Nazareth in that week before the journey to Jerusalem during those last services before the pilgrimage, services filled with all the anxieties and ardors of Israel—as well as the still hidden germs of Christian spirituality.

Then comes the *Shema* whose opening verse has already been quoted. Every Jew must recite this verse daily: as he rises and as he retires for the night Jesus, according to the Gospel of Mark, considered it one of the two fundamentals of the Law, a verse of the greatest importance. But it should not be considered apart from what follows it. The *Shema* is not only a religious affirmation or a profession of faith; it implies a rule of life and is a reliving of the past. For Israel the past is always a present experience, and in this sense it is always preparing the future.

Each service in the synagogue and in the Temple will present to the young Jesus the unfolding totality of the *Shema* as God has given it in the Bible. It is composed of three fragments of the Pentateuch joined together, three episodes of the revelation of the Law at Sinai.

Here is the first fragment, taken from Deuteronomy and accompanied, for liturgical purposes, by a blessing. It includes the words with which Moses, after proclaiming the Law, specified the practical means by which the Chosen People would preserve it and spread it among the nations.

Hear, O Israel: The Lord is our God, the Lord is one.
Blessed be his name, whose glorious kingdom is for ever and
ever.

You shall love Yahweh your God with all your heart, with
all your soul, with all your strength. Let these words I urge on
you today be written on your heart. You shall repeat them to
your children and say them over to them whether at rest in
your house or walking abroad, at your lying down or at your
rising: you shall fasten them on your hand as a sign and on
your forehead as a circlet; you shall write them on the door-
posts of your house and on your gates (Dt. 6:4-9).

After this repetition of the instruction inspired by God more
than a thousand years before, the young Jesus, standing
beside his father, must have repeated the sacred prayer in a
quiet voice. With the whole congregation he then continued
with a later passage in Deuteronomy found at verses 13-21 of
chapter eleven. This forms the second part of the *Shema*.

Jesus knows that these are not just phrases: they entail certain gestures and actions. Hence Joseph taught him to recite
morning and evening, the initial verse of the *Shema*, in
obedience to the command: "You will teach these to your
children." These words will be repeated several times a day in
the home, and also during the coming journey to Jerusalem.
This journey haunts the imagination, for the instruction is,
"You will repeat them in your house and on a journey." So
too, the first verse of the *Shema* is written indelibly on a piece
of parchment and placed in a small leather case attached to the
left arm of each believer as well as to the middle of his
forehead. It is also placed in a wooden tube or reed called a
mezuza which is attached to the posts of the entrance and inner
doors of the house. (These precepts, however constraining and
inconvenient they may be, must be observed religiously.)

The second paragraph of the *Shema* speaks of the dreaded
choice between obedience and disobedience which must be

made by the community of Israel as a whole and by each Jew
in particular who stands as a link in the history of that community.

Again, it is Moses' words directly inspired by God that
come to the lips of Jesus or sound in his ears:

> . . . And it is most sure that if you faithfully obey the com-
> mandments I enjoin on you today, loving Yahweh your God
> and serving him with all your heart and all your soul, "I will
> give your land rain in season, autumn rain and spring, so that
> you may harvest your corn, your wine, your oil; I shall
> provide grass in the fields for your cattle, and you will eat and
> have all you want." Take care your heart is not seduced, that
> you do not go astray, serving other gods and worshipping
> them, or the anger of Yahweh will blaze out against you, he
> will shut up the heavens and there will be no rain, the land
> will not yield its produce and you will quickly die in the pros-
> perous land that Yahweh is giving you.

> Let these words of mine remain in your heart and in your
> soul; fasten them on your hand as a sign and on your forehead
> as a circlet. Teach them to your children and say them over to
> them, whether at rest in your house or walking abroad, at
> your lying down or at your rising. Write them on the door-
> posts of your house and on your gates, so that you and your
> children may live long in the land that Yahweh swore to your
> fathers he would give them for as long as there is a sky above
> the earth (Dt. 11:13-21).

One ought not to hear these promises and threats as though
they were addressed simply to individuals who would be
tempted then to receive them in a superstitious or mercenary
way. Such an interpretation would be too facile, and unworthy
of *Adonai emeth*, the "God of Truth." And as the Book of Job
suggests, it is quite unnecessary for God to give reasons for
his chastisement of his creatures. Rather one should hear these
promises and threats of the *Shema* as addressed to the entire
nation of Israel representing humanity. There is no reason for

any given individual to believe that observance of the *Shema* will cause rain to fall on his field in time of drought. Yet it is certain that in alternating periods of drought and rain, of scarcity and abundance, the priestly people of God will survive throughout the centuries, along with the human race whose servants they are, providing they remain faithful to the law of Sinai and observe the *Shema*. This promise is no simple opium for individuals or even for the people; it is an existential truth as it has been for 3,500 years.

The third paragraph of the *Shema* repeats the words of the Lord giving Moses and the children of Israel a specific means of remembering his law. Here is taught the use of *tsitsith*, the woolen threads added to the fringes of clothing.

> *Yahweh spoke to Moses and said, "Speak to the sons of Israel and tell them to put tassels on the hems of their garments, and to put a violet cord on this tassel at the hem. You must have a tassel, then, and the sight of it will remind you of all the commands of Yahweh. You are to put them into practice then, and no longer follow the desires of your heart and your eyes, which have led you to make wantons of yourselves.*

> *This will remind you of all my commandments; put them into practice, and you will be consecrated to your God. It is I, Yahweh your God, who have brought you out of the land of Egypt so that I may be your God, I, Yahweh, your God"* (Nb. 15:37-41).

As he hears the ten verses of the Decalogue and the three paragraphs of the *Shema* that follow this proclamation of the oneness of God, Jesus now becomes familiar with the essence of the message entrusted by God to Israel, and he experiences the religious atmosphere in which his people live.

The precepts taught him by the service celebrated in the village synagogue are not abstract or theoretical; liturgy is not detached from life; his call is not to a transcendence reserved for initiates or for the clerics of an official cult, as is the case among pagans.

Two-thirds of the Decalogue concerns unbelievers as well as believers, idolaters as well as Jews. All are carried along by the same Providence towards the coming, or at least the advance, of the Kingdom of God on earth. Much of the *Shema* gives practical advice on making perceptible the revealed word of God. The exalted opening verse leads into minute rulings applying to everyday, even banal, aspects of man's life on earth, his lodging, clothing, etc. Jesus could not fail to realize, with perhaps considerable wonder, that there was no distinction, no separation between the secular and the sacred, between the laity and the religious.

Following the *Shema* in the synagogue service come the liturgical benedictions. Even though they differ from those which accompany daily life, they use the same initial formula. These are silent blessings, introduced by the celebrant, and were six in number at the time of Jesus. Together they form what is called *Amidah*, which is spoken softly, standing:

> *O Lord, open thou my lips, and my mouth shall declare thy praise.*

> *Blessed art thou, O Lord our God and God of our fathers, God of Abraham, God of Isaac, and God of Jacob, the great, mighty and revered God, the most high God, who bestowest loving kindness, and art Master of all things; who rememberest the pious deeds of the patriarchs, and in love wilt bring a redeemer to their children's children for thy Name's sake.*

> *   *   *   *   *

> *O King, Helper, Saviour and Shield. Blessed art thou, O Lord, the Shield of Abraham.*

> *Thou, O Lord, art mighty for ever, thou revivest the dead, thou art mighty to save.*

Thou sustainest the living with loving kindness, revivest the dead with great mercy, supportest the falling, healest the sick, freest the bound, and keepest thy faith to them that sleep in the dust. Who is like unto thee, Lord of mighty acts, and who resembleth thee, O King, who orderest death and restorest life, and causest salvation to spring forth?

*   *   *   *   *

Thou art holy, and thy Name is holy, and the holy praise thee daily. (Selah.) Blessed art thou, O Lord, the holy God.

*   *   *   *   *

Towards the righteous and the pious, towards the elders of thy people the house of Israel, towards the remnant of their scribes, towards true proselytes, and towards us also may thy tender mercies be stirred, O Lord our God: grant a good reward unto all who faithfully trust in thy Name; set our portion with them for ever, so that we may not be put to shame; for we have trusted in thee. Blessed art thou, O Lord, the stay and trust of the righteous.

*   *   *   *   *

Hear our voice, O Lord our God; spare us and have mercy upon us, and accept our prayer in mercy and favour; for thou art a God who hearkenest unto prayers and supplications: from thy presence, O our King, turn us not away; for thou hearkenest to the prayer of thy people Israel. Blessed art thou, O Lord, who hearkenest unto prayer.

*   *   *   *   *

We give thanks unto thee, for thou art the Lord our God and the God of our fathers for ever and ever; thou art the Rock of our lives, the Shield of our salvation through every generation. We will give thanks unto thee and declare thy praise for our lives which are committed unto thy hand, and for our souls which are in thy charge, and for thy miracles, which are daily with us, and for thy wonders and thy benefits,

> *which are wrought at all times, evening, morn and noon. . .*
> (ADPB, *pp. 131, 133, 135, 137, 145, 147, 151*).

After these blessings have been said silently and repeated aloud, then come the actual prayers. Two recited in the course of the service are basic. One is the *Kaddish*, which is an antecedent of the Christian "Our Father." It was written in literary Aramaic, the language of intellectuals at the time of Jesus, and not in Hebrew, the language of the liturgy. It has been modified through the centuries, but it has always formed part of the service. The congregation stood for its recitation.

> *Magnified and sanctified be his great Name in the world which he hath created according to his will. May he establish his kingdom during your life and during your days, and during the life of all the house of Israel, even speedily and at a near time, and say ye, Amen.*
>
> *Let his great Name be blessed for ever and to all eternity.*
>
> *Blessed, praised and fortified, exalted, extolled and honoured, magnified and lauded be the Name of the Holy One, blessed be he; though he be high above all the blessings and hymns, praises and consolations, which are uttered in the world; and say ye, Amen.*
>
> *May there be abundant peace from heaven, and life for us and for all Israel; and say ye, Amen.*
>
> *He who maketh peace in his high places, may he make peace for us and for all Israel; and say ye, Amen* (ADPB, *p. 213*).

The service ends with the *Oleynu*, a prayer declaring the oneness of God and entrusting the Jews with its proclamation on earth.

> *It is our duty to praise the Lord of all things, to ascribe*

greatness to him who formed the world in the beginning, since he hath not made us like the nations of other lands, and hath not placed us like other families of the earth, since he hath not assigned unto us a portion as unto them, nor a lot as unto all their multitude. For we bend the knee and offer worship and thanks before the supreme King of kings, the Holy One, blessed be he who stretched forth the heavens and laid the foundations of the earth, the seat of whose glory is in the heavens above, and the abode of whose might is in the loftiest heights. He is our God; there is none else: in truth he is our King; there is none besides him; as it is written in his Torah, And thou shalt know this day, and lay it to thine heart, that the Lord he is God in heaven above and upon the earth beneath: there is none else.

We therefore hope in thee, O Lord our God, that we may speedily behold the glory of thy might, when thou wilt remove the abominations from the earth, and heathendom will be utterly destroyed, when the world will be perfected under the kingdom of the Almighty, and all the children of flesh will call upon thy Name, when thou wilt turn unto thyself all the evildoers upon earth. Let all the inhabitants of the world perceive and know that unto thee every knee must bow, every tongue must swear allegiance. Before thee, O Lord our God, let them bow and worship; and unto thy glorious Name let them give honour; let them all accept the yoke of thy kingdom, and do thou reign over them speedily, and for ever and ever. For the kingdom is thine, and to all eternity thou wilt reign in glory; as it is written in thy Torah, "The Lord shall reign for ever and ever," and it is said, "And the Lord shall be king over all the earth: in that day shall the Lord be one and his name one" (ADPB, p. 299).

This describes in essence the Friday evening service which begins the Sabbath.

As soon as the service is over the congregation, after exchanging the usual salutation, *Shabbat Shalom,* "Peace and happiness for the Sabbath," leave the synagogue and return home.

Their walk home along the narrow lanes of Nazareth may follow a familiar path amongst the closely crowded houses, nothing unusual meeting the eye; and yet everything is new, for this walk is celebrating the advent of a sacred time. On their way Joseph may remind Jesus of a fable recorded later in the Talmud: "Two angels, one good, one wicked, on the eve of the Sabbath, accompany each Jew from the synagogue to his home. If the Sabbath lamp is lit and the table set, the good angel prays that the same be true on the following Sabbath, and the bad angel is compelled to say: 'Amen.' But if nothing has been done to prepare for the Sabbath, the bad angel utters a curse, and the good angel is obliged to say: 'Amen.'"

Fortunately, Joseph and Jesus see that all is well, that Mary has prepared everything for the family celebration. The bad angel will say "Amen." Their house, a simple one, is open now to the majesty of God. It is adorned to welcome the Sabbath with the joy and anticipation with which one prepares to receive a beloved and lovely lady. The Sabbath liturgy and family conversation refer to the Sabbath as "Queen" and "fiancée." It is welcomed with words of love, recalling the Song of Songs, that extraordinary biblical book of passion and holiness. In later centuries the lyrical expectation of the Sabbath will be expressed in one of the synagogue hymns which have been part of the Friday evening service since the sixteenth century: "Lekha Dodi . . . Come my beloved, with chorus of praise, Welcome Bride Sabbath, the Queen of the days" (ADPB, p. 357). In such a spirit did each house welcome the Sabbath.

Faithful families have now put on their festive clothing. They have decorated their homes and made their tables lovely. All are eager to honor this day of serenity and joy when cares and sadness are banished, all mourning suspended, when relatives and friends gather in special intimacy and love radiates from the humblest homes and most sumptuous dwellings.

The Sabbath is the only day that belongs entirely to God. The Lord was himself the first to observe it, and his example teaches us that all work, no matter how important, must cease as the seventh day draws near. And it worked out very well that way, for on the evening of the sixth day—according to an ancient tradition—God was on the point of creating bodies for devils whose souls he had already fashioned. Fortunately the Sabbath began and prevented him from carrying out his design. So it is these devils who sometimes lodge in the hearts of men; having no bodies they remain invisible.

It has been said that the patriarchs observed the Sabbath even before the revelation at Sinai. But the Sabbath became part of the life of the people of Israel and of every individual Jew only after the proclamation of the Law by Moses on the mountain. From that time on it became not only an obligatory day of rest but above all a day of joy. According to the *Haggadah*, the Sabbath must be received both as a precious gift from Heaven (*Mathana tovah*) and as a day of delight (*Oneg Shabbat*).

> *If you refrain from trampling the sabbath,*
> *and doing business on the holy day,*
> *if you call the sabbath "Delightful"*
> *and the day sacred to Yahweh "Honourable,"*
> *if you honour it by abstaining from travel,*
> *from doing business and from gossip,*
> *then shall you find your happiness in Yahweh*
> *and I will lead you triumphant over the heights of the land.*
> *I will feed you on the heritage of Jacob your father.*
> *For the mouth of Yahweh has spoken (Is. 58:13-14).*

The Sabbath is a foretaste of the world to come, for on that day one enjoys a sixtieth part of the delights of the afterlife—not much when compared to eternal happiness, but appreciable when compared to the happiness of earth!

And so each week, from sundown on Friday to nightfall on Saturday, the Jew refrains from any work. Agriculture and commerce are forbidden; it is also forbidden to write or to travel, to build fires or to do household chores. All the needs of the holy day have been attended to the day before.

This day of inactivity applies also to slaves and servants, as is stated in the Decalogue:

> *Remember the sabbath day and keep it holy. For six days you shall labour and do all your work, but the seventh day is a sabbath for the Lord your God. You shall do no work that day, neither you nor your son, nor your daughter, nor your servants, men or women, nor your animals, nor the stranger who lives with you. For in six days the Lord made the heavens and the earth and the sea and all that these hold, but on the seventh day he rested; that is why the Lord has blessed the sabbath day and made it sacred (Ex. 20:8-11).*

The Sabbath day is unique. According to tradition, this is built into the very structure of the week. Each day is linked to another, the first to the second, the third to the fourth, the fifth to the sixth; but the seventh day, the Sabbath, stands alone. When in the beginning, the Sabbath complained to God at being thus unmatched and neglected, the Lord explained the reason for such a fate. Israel, which observes the Sabbath isolated among other days, is also a people isolated among other nations, the special and solitary companion of God.

One can see then the singular importance of the observance of the Sabbath. A tradition already extant at the time of Jesus and with which he must have been familiar, declares that if the whole of Israel observed two successive Sabbaths as they should be observed, the redemption of all humanity would be accomplished. This means that the perfect observance of two Sabbaths would be enough to bring the Kingdom of God. If the people of Israel, however, were incapable of such an effort, but could simply observe one Sabbath without negligence or alteration, then the Messiah would appear to usher in the kingdom.

As a contemporary rabbi has written, this day is a continuation of the adventure begun with Abraham, and it is linked with the fate of the whole of creation. Another rabbi gives this

final counsel which sums up the seriousness and the joy of the
Sabbath: "Serve God in fear and rejoice in trembling."

The beginning of these joyous home festivities is the *Kiddush*,
a ceremony celebrated by Joseph with the help of Mary, and in
the presence of the young Jesus, as soon as they are home
again. That meal, like all meals served at Jewish tables, con-
forms to the dietary rules laid down by God for his people.
Some were originally intended to protect their health, the distinction between pure and impure meats being for the sake of
hygiene. In general what would today be called red meats are
allowed, and the others forbidden. Deuteronomy prescribes
thus:

> These are the animals you may eat: ox, sheep, goat, deer,
> gazelle, roebuck, ibex, antelope, oryx, mountain sheep. You
> may eat any animal that has a divided and cloven hoof and
> that is a ruminant. Of those, however, that are ruminant and
> those that have a divided and cloven hoof you may not eat the
> following: the camel, the hare and the hyrax, which are rumi-
> nant but have no cloven hoof; you must hold them unclean.
> So also the pig, which though it has a cloven hoof is not rumi-
> nant; you must hold it unclean. You must not eat the meat of
> such animals nor touch their dead bodies (Dt. 14:4-8).

Does not this "diet" required by God recall prescriptions
given by our modern physicians?

The Bible even at that time believed that food which is impure can contaminate food which is pure. The rabbinical tradition illustrates this: "If an impure or forbidden object falls into
a pot containing food authorized by the Law, the whole contents of the pot is forbidden, unless no taste of the forbidden
object can be detected in the contents of the pot." Can we not
see in the writing of this Talmudic rabbi the beginning of an-
tiseptic hygiene such as is practiced today?

But there are other reasons greater in number and more essential, and of a religious nature. Some have their origin in

historical events related in the Bible. For instance, if it is forbidden to eat the sciatic nerve of an animal, this is for a reason
described in Genesis (Jacob wrestling with the Angel):

> [*And the angel*] *struck him in the socket of his hip, and*
> *Jacob's hip was dislocated as he wrestled with him . . . That is*
> *the reason why to this day the Israelites do not eat the sciatic*
> *nerve which is in the socket of the hip; because he had struck*
> *Jacob in the socket of the hip on the sciatic nerve (Gn.: 32:25,*
> *33).*

But most of these rules stem from deep-seated beliefs basic to
the piety of the time. If it is forbidden to consume blood under
any form, and if one must therefore kill animals in such a way
as to draw their blood away, it is because blood contains the
vital element of being, and in consuming it, one would
become changed, even identified with the deceased animal.
"All the fat belongs to Yahweh. This is a perpetual law for all
your descendants, wherever you may live: never eat either fat
or blood" (Lv. 3:17). And Genesis specifies:" . . . you must not
eat flesh with life, that is to say blood in it" (Gn. 9:5).

To cook a kid in the milk of its mother would also be an
affront to natural law and respect for life. The Pentateuch in-
sists three times on this interdiction.

Such are some of the food ordinances which the housewife
must follow in the preparation of the meal. Mary may have observed them more scrupulously than usual as the Sabbath
began, since in her family it was never a question of merely
conforming to meticulous regulations. They know that all
these ordinances originate in the priestly vocation of the
Hebrew people. A passage from Leviticus witnesses to this:

> *For it is I, Yahweh, who am your God. You have been sanc-*
> *tified and have become holy because I am holy: do not defile*
> *yourself with all these beasts that crawl on the ground. Yes, it*
> *is I, Yahweh, who brought you out of Egypt to be your God:*
> *you therefore must be holy because I am holy (Lv. 11:44-45).*

To this very clear text a treatise from the Talmud adds these details:

> *This is the teaching concerning quadrupeds, winged creatures, creatures that live in the waters and that crawl upon the earth, in order that one may distinguish the pure from the impure, and those that may be eaten from those that may not be eaten.*

So as he sits at the family table for this first meal of the Sabbath Jesus takes part in the observance of the Law and in the vocation of his people Israel.

Joseph as head of the family lifts a cup of wine, symbol of life and joy, and praises God whose presence at the table he celebrates for the gift of the Sabbath. And the next day, when the sacred time comes to an end, a similar ceremony but inverted, the *Havdolah* ("separation"), will mark the end of the Sabbath and the beginning of the secular week. At that time the blessing of the wine will be accompanied by a meditation on a fragrant plant and on a burning lamp. But now as the Sabbath begins Joseph and Jesus sit at table, and Joseph, holding the cup filled with wine, says the usual prayers and blessings:

> *And it was the sixth day.*

> *And the heaven and the earth were finished and all their host. And on the seventh day God had finished his work which he had made. And God blessed the seventh day, and he hallowed it, because he rested thereon from all his work which God had created and made (ADPB, p. 381).*

> *Blessed art thou, O Lord our God, King of the universe, who createst the fruit of the vine (Ibid., p. 395).*

> *Blessed art thou, O Lord our God, King of the universe, who hast hallowed us by thy commandments and hast taken pleasure in us, and in love and favour hast given us thy holy*

> *Sabbath as an inheritance, a memorial of the creation—that*
> *day being also the first of the holy convocations, in remem-*
> *brance of the departure from Egypt. For thou hast chosen us*
> *and hallowed us above all nations, and in love and favour hast*
> *given us thy holy Sabbath as an inheritance. Blessed art thou,*
> *O Lord, who hallowest the Sabbath* (Ibid.).

Then Joseph says another blessing, this time over the bread. Two whole loaves are laid on the table, one over the other, to commemorate the double ration of manna which fell from heaven. Joseph breaks the loaf which is underneath and distributes a piece to each of those present, who declare as they eat: "Blessed art thou, O Lord our God, King of the universe, who bringest forth bread from the earth" (*Ibid.*, p. 409).

The meal now takes place, a meal like any other, though perhaps a little more elaborate and abundant than usual. Is it not traditional to eat nothing on Friday afternoon in order to save one's appetite for the evening? A meal like any other—but the wine and the bread, although no different from the wine and the bread taken during the week, have both been consecrated to God by the blessing of men.

As soon as the meal is over, Joseph chants Psalm 126 in the presence of Mary and Jesus:

> *When Yahweh brought Zion's captives home,*
> *   at first it seemed like a dream;*
> *then our mouths filled with laughter*
> *   and our lips with song.*
>
> *Even the pagans started talking*
> *   about the marvels the Lord had done for us!*
> *What marvels indeed he did for us,*
> *   and how overjoyed we were!*
>
> *Yahweh, bring all our captives back again*
> *   like torrents in the Negeb!*
> *Those who went sowing in tears*
> *   now sing as they reap.*

They went away, went away weeping,
  carrying the seed;
they come back, come back singing,
  carrying their sheaves.

Then grace is said, with the following introduction which depends for its form on the number of persons present. If there are at least three men gathered around the table, the recitation must be out loud. The leader takes a glass of wine and says:

Blessed be the name of the Lord from this time forth and for-ever. We will bless him of whose bounty we have partaken. Blessed be he of whose bounty we have partaken. Blessed be he, and blessed be his name (Ibid., p. 965–7).

If there are fewer than three men, one says: "Blessed art thou, O Lord our God, King of the universe, who feedest the whole world with thy goodness" (*Ibid.*, p. 967).

Then grace begins:

. . . with grace, with loving kindness and tender mercy; thou givest food to all flesh, for thy loving kindness endureth for ever. Through thy great goodness food hath never failed us: O may it not fail us for ever and ever for thy great Name's sake, since thou nourishest and sustainest all beings, and doest good unto all, and providest food for all thy creatures whom thou hast created. Blessed art thou, O Lord, who givest food unto all.

We thank thee, O Lord our God, because thou didst give as an heritage unto our fathers a desirable, good and ample land, and because thou didst bring us forth, O Lord our God, from the land of Egypt, and didst deliver us from the house of bond-age; as well as for thy covenant which thou hast sealed in our flesh, thy Torah which thou hast taught us, thy statutes which thou hast bestowed upon us, and for the food wherewith thou dost constantly feed and sustain us on every day, in every season, at every hour (Ibid., pp. 967, 969).

When the meal is over, Jesus and his family retire for the
night. Besides the usual prayers, the *Shema*, which every Jew
says in the evening, Joseph recites the *Hashkivenu*, a prayer
asking for the blessing of God upon their sleep and peace
throughout the night.

> *Cause us, O Lord our God, to lie down in peace, and raise*
> *us up, O our King, unto life. Spread over us the protection of*
> *thy peace; direct us aright through thine own good counsel;*
> *save us for thy Name's sake; be thou a shield about us; remove*
> *from us every enemy, pestilence, sword, famine and sorrow;*
> *remove also the adversary from before us and from behind us.*
> *O shelter us beneath the shadow of thy wings; for thou, O*
> *God, art our Guardian and our Deliverer; yea, thou, O God,*
> *art a gracious and merciful King; and guard our going and our*
> *coming unto life and unto peace from this time forth and for*
> *evermore; yea, spread over us the protection of thy peace.*
> *Blessed art thou, O Lord, who spreadest the protection of thy*
> *peace. Blessed art thou, O Lord, who spreadest the protection*
> *of peace over us and over all thy people Israel, and over*
> *Jerusalem* (Ibid., p. 373).

The next day at dawn Jesus and Joseph return to the synagogue. The service which will take place is the most complete
and important of the Sabbath, for it includes the ceremonies
attendant upon the reading of the Law when the tabernacle is
opened and the scrolls are brought out. On this solemn occasion which emphasizes the priestly character of the whole
people of Israel and of each Jew in particular, everyone must
wrap himself in the prayer shawl, the *tallith*.

The *tallith* is a ritual cloak which evokes the prehistoric days
of the religion of Israel. When the ancestors of the Jews were
nomadic shepherds, they wore *abayah*, blankets of white wool
adorned with black stripes at both ends, to protect them from
the sun and rain.

As successive revelations further defined the vocation of
Israel, the wearing of this primitive garment took on a

religious meaning, as was the case with so many other customs. The Torah explains its sacred character. This sanctification of the shawls of the old nomads is first found in the Book of Numbers. The Lord ordered them to add *tsitsith*, fringes braided of white and colored threads, to their shawls to remind them of its religious significance. The *tsitsith* remind Jews of the divine order and of the commandments of the Torah.

As the Lord says again in the last book of the Pentateuch: "You are to make tassels for the four corners of the cloak in which you wrap yourself" (Dt. 22:12).

Two of the leading rabbis of Jesus' time differed on the making of these fringes. According to the school of *Shammai*, which always carried ritualistic rules to extremes, each *tsitsith* should be made of four threads of white wool and four threads of blue. According to the school of Hillel, always more liberal, two threads of each color were sufficient.

Like the phylacteries on the head and the arms, or the *mezuza* on the door of the house, the *tsitsith* on their clothing are a loving gift from God to his people, Israel. They are an essential part of the ritual clothing of the Jew by which he is distinguished from the Gentile. A result of this is that a Jew is not allowed to sell a garment trimmed with fringes to a non-Jew unless he first removes them.

A fable recorded in the Talmud and which undoubtedly was part of the oral tradition at the time of Jesus' childhood, describes the world to come and the rewards that pious Jews will receive for their fidelity. A Jew who has observed the Law, and in particular, the commandment regarding the *tsitsith*, will be attended by an enormous number of companions, no less than 2,800. Where does this huge figure come from, and how is it explained? As always, it is by interpreting a biblical text that one arrives at an answer.

> *The Lord God says this. In those days, ten men of nations of every language will take a Jew by the sleeve and say, "We want to go with you, since we have learnt that God is with you"(Zc. 8:23).*

Considering that there are seventy different languages on earth and that there are four corners to which the *tsitsith* are attached, one obtains the figure 2,800 — the minimum number of voluntary attendants who commit themselves to following a Jew who has complied with the Law.

This fable, like most of those found in the rabbinic tradition, and perhaps even those found in the Gospels, originates in the Semitic mind, which is not limited by the need for accuracy and objectivity. It must not, therefore, be taken literally. What matters is not the exact number but the meaning. To speak of 2,800 men accompanying each pious Jew is merely a way of saying that the Jew is responsible for the fate of a great number of his contemporaries. Israel has a deep belief in the influence a just man can exert. Through his actions, through his obedience to the Law, he contributes to establishing order in the world and to preparing for the coming of the Kingdom of God. "A sin," the rabbis say, "is a break in the harmony of the world, and a good deed is a reparation." A man who lives according to the Law is never isolated from the world. The destinies of thousands of his brothers depend upon him.

There is another fable in the Talmud which shows the power of the *tsitsith*. On one occasion a mystic (*hassid*) was tempted sensually, tormented by the flesh. The *tsitsith* acted as living witnesses, slapped him on the face "as a reproach to him," and turned him away from temptation.

The blue threads on the fringe are more significant than the white. "Why a blue thread?" a rabbi asked one day. He was told: "Because that color resembles the sea; because the sea resembles the sky, and the sky resembles the seat of divine glory where, they say, under God's feet is a stone of sapphire."

But how was the color blue obtained at the time of Jesus? The Talmud once more gives us the answer, but it is allegorical rather than literal. Its purpose is to exalt the color chosen. The Talmud informs us that the color was produced by dyeing the fringes with the blood of a kind of snail or a shellfish — half real, half legendary, called the *hamzun* — which supposedly appeared only once every seventy years. In other words at the time of Jesus when the oral tradition, the *Mishnah*, which inspired the Talmud, had not yet been written down, the *hamzun* was so rare that the religious authorities took into account the difficulty of collecting its blood and decided that only threads of white were necessary. Consequently a Talmudic rabbi remarks that the punishment for dispensing with white threads should be heavier than the punishment for dispensing with blue threads. This same doctor, in order to be understood, uses a simile: a king, he says, orders one of his servants to procure an earthen seal, and another to procure a gold one. Both fail in their mission. The king punishes the first one more severely for failing to achieve his simple and easy task than the second, since he recognizes the differing circumstances.

So even in the case of the *tsitsith*, this special symbol of Jewish piety, tradition can be lenient and take special cases into account.

The *tallith* in which Joseph and Jesus wrap themselves are very much like those of the shepherds of old. They are made of the unbleached, rough wool from the lambs that graze in the fields of Palestine. *Tallith* are long, sometimes reaching the ankles, as if to protect the whole body from the influence of idolatry and doubt, and are made of two lengths of material sewn together. Without ornament or refinement, they are easy to distinguish from the silk prayer shawls which resemble the Roman pallium. They were worn by city-dwellers influenced by Latin culture. Jesus must have met many of those in the Temple.

On this occasion at Nazareth, Jesus watches Joseph putting on his prayer shawl. He wraps it round his head and throws both ends over his left shoulder, so that the four corners may be together.

Joseph whispers the prayer of sanctification inspired by Numbers:

Beschem Adonai . . . *In the Name of God the Holy One,*

whose oneness is acknowledged by all Israel. I am going to put
on the tallith *adorned with the* tsitsith *in order to fulfill the*
command of my Creator: "You and your descendants are to
make tassels for the four corners of your cloak" (Dt. 22:12;
Nb. 15:37-41).

Then he uncovers his head, lays the shawl over his shoulders
and says the first blessing which marks his participation in the
Saturday morning service: "Blessed art thou, O Lord our God,
King of the universe, who hast hallowed us by thy commandments and hast commanded us to enwrap ourselves in the
fringed garment" (*ADPB*, p. 45).

As Jesus watches Joseph carrying out these traditional gestures, speaking words directly inspired by God, he realizes
that the humble village carpenter is exercising his priestly dignity.

What an amazing sight! An ordinary inhabitant of Nazareth,
a modest Jewish artisan, becoming a link in the divine action,
uninterrupted for 1,500 years, and this without renouncing
any aspect of his daily life. By his liturgical action and speech
he echoes the words which God used in giving his Law to the
world. In one year, as Jesus knows, he will himself carry out
the same gestures and participate in the priesthood of Israel.

The New Testament confirms the fact that Jesus observed
the law in his wearing of the *tsitsith*: "From behind him came
a woman—and she touched the fringe of his cloak" (Mt. 9:20).

By this gesture so characteristic of Jewish piety the woman
was honoring the priestly vocation which Jesus, son of Israel,
took upon himself in accordance with the teaching of the
Torah.

Then begins the Saturday morning service, the climax of the
Sabbath. Much of it is still in use today. Besides the main
blessings and prayers common to all services, this service has
the following eight parts:

Three Psalms: 19, 90, 145;
The *Nishmat kol haï,* a hymn of praise;

the bringing out of the Law and the reading of the
  Torah;
the priestly blessing;
the prayer for the congregation;
the reading of a passage from the Prophets, called the
  Haftorah.

In the Psalms and hymns of praise, which are preparation
for the crucial moment of the reading of the Law, the people
express their unity with God who gave them the Torah. The
Psalms recall the most exalted moments in the history of Israel
and the personalities who dominated it: Moses of Sinai and
David, King of Israel, who first conceived the Temple.

All the great moments of Jewish history are thus mentioned
at the climax of the liturgy, when the *Sefer Torah* is taken out
of the tabernacle. Here are the introductory lines chanted by
the celebrant and answered antiphonally by Jesus and the
whole congregation. First, Psalm 19 consecrated to the Sabbath:

> *The heavens declare the glory of God,*
> *the vault of heaven proclaims his handiwork:*
> *day discourses of it to day,*
> *night to night hands on the knowledge.*
>
> *No utterance at all, no speech,*
> *no sound that anyone can hear;*
> *yet their voice goes out through all the earth,*
> *and their message to the ends of the world.*
>
> *High above, he pitched a tent for the sun,*
> *who comes out of his pavilion like a bridegroom,*
> *exulting like a hero to run his race.*
>
> *He has his rising on the edge of heaven,*
> *the end of his course is its furthest edge,*
> *and nothing can escape his heat.*

The Law of Yahweh is perfect,
  new life for the soul;
the decree of Yahweh is trustworthy,
  wisdom for the simple.

The precepts of Yahweh are upright,
  joy for the heart;
the commandment of Yahweh is clear,
  light for the eyes.

The fear of Yahweh is pure,
  lasting for ever;
the judgements of Yahweh are true,
  righteous, every one,

more desirable than gold,
  even than the finest gold;
his words are sweeter than honey,
  even than honey that drips from the comb.

Thus your servant is formed by them,
  observance brings great reward.
But who can detect his own failings?
  Wash out my hidden faults.

And from pride preserve your servant,
  never let it dominate me.
So shall I be above reproach,
  free from grave sin.

May the words of my mouth always find favour,
  and the whispering of my heart,
in your presence, Yahweh,
  my Rock, my Redeemer:

Next, Psalm 90: a Prayer of Moses, man of God:

Lord, you have been
our refuge age after age.

Before the mountains were born,
before the earth or the world came to birth,
you were God from all eternity and for ever.

You can turn man back into dust
by saying, 'Back to what you were, you sons of men!'
To you, a thousand years are a single day,
a yesterday now over, an hour of the night.

You brush men away like waking dreams,
they are like grass
sprouting and flowering in the morning,
withered and dry before dusk.

We too are burnt up by your anger
and terrified by your fury;
having summoned up our sins
you inspect our secrets by your own light.

Our days dwindle under your wrath,
our lives are over in a breath
—our life lasts for seventy years,
eighty with good health,

but they all add up to anxiety and trouble—
over in a trice, and then we are gone.
Who yet has felt the full force of your fury,
or learnt to fear the violence of your rage?

Teach us to count how few days we have
and so gain wisdom of heart.
Relent, Yahweh! How much longer do we have?
Take pity on your servants!

Let us wake in the morning filled with your love
and sing and be happy all our days;
make our future as happy as our past was sad,
those years when you were punishing us.

Let your servants see what you can do for them,
let their children see your glory.
May the sweetness of the Lord be on us!
Make all we do succeed.

The last, Psalm 145, is a hymn of David praising the Lord:

I sing your praises, God my King,
I bless your name for ever and ever,
blessing you day after day,
and praising your name for ever and ever.
Can anyone measure the magnificence
of Yahweh the great, and his inexpressible grandeur?

Celebrating your acts of power,
one age shall praise your doings to another.
Oh, the splendour of your glory, your renown!
I tell myself the story of your marvellous deeds. . .

    *   *   *   *   *

Yahweh's praise be ever in my mouth,
and let every creature bless his holy name
for ever and ever!

The *Nishmat kol haï* comes next, a hymn of praise, the main parts of which go back to earliest times:

The breath of every living being shall bless thy Name, O Lord our God, and the spirit of all flesh shall ever extol and exalt thy fame, O our King. From everlasting to everlasting thou art God; and beside thee we have no King, O thou who redeemest and savest, settest free and deliverest, who supportest and pitiest in all times of trouble and distress; yea, we have no King but thee.

Thou art God of the first and of the last ages, God of all creatures, Lord of all generations, adored in innumerable praises, guiding thy world with loving kindness and thy creatures with tender mercies. The Lord slumbereth not, nor sleepeth; he arouseth the sleepers and awakeneth the slumberers; he maketh the dumb to speak, setteth free the prisoners, supporteth the falling, and raiseth up those who are bowed down.

To thee alone we give thanks. . . . Thou didst redeem us from Egypt, O Lord our God, and didst release us from the house of bondage; . . . Who is like unto thee, who is equal to thee, who can be compared unto thee, O God, great, mighty, and awful, most high God, Maker of heaven and earth? We will praise, laud and glorify thee, and we will bless thy holy Name, as it is said, "Bless the Lord, O my soul, and all that is within me bless his holy name "(ADPB, pp. 417, 419, 421).

The ceremony of the bringing out of the Law is the most majestic of all. The entire continuity of Israel is celebrated at this moment. The liturgy in its every gesture and detail prepares for the stupendous event to be reenacted.

The platform of the synagogue, the *tebah,* becomes once more the holy mountain upon which God gave his Law to the world through Moses.

This is the solemn prayer recited in front of the tabernacle just before it is opened to bring forth the scrolls of the Law. It is made in the name of the whole community and expresses the reverence and the emotion of all the faithful:

God of the spirits of all flesh, we come before the tabernacle of the Law, the heritage of Israel, filled with profound reverence and awe.

Though infinity is thy temple, and the world which thou hast formed is the altar of thy glory, yet thou hast chosen the heart of man wherein to raise up a sanctuary for thine adoration by prayer pure and fervent.

*Deign, O Lord, to fill our thoughts with thy spirit and so to
purify them that they may be worthy of the worship we offer,
for a clear conscience is the finest offering, and repentance the
truest prayer.*

*As we bow our faces before thine ineffable majesty, and lift
up from the depths of our hearts our prayer to thee, towards
thy magnificent throne, we pray thee to inspire us to noble
and holy deeds, to the glory of thy Name. Amen.*

The tabernacle is then opened with a song of joy and of confidence in the eternal Lord Sabaoth:

*As the ark set out, Moses would say, "Arise, Yahweh, may
your enemies be scattered and those who hate you run for their
lives before you!" (Nb. 10:35). The Law will go out from Zion,
and the oracle of Yahweh from Jerusalem (Is. 2:3).*

*Gates, raise your arches,
rise you ancient doors,
let the king of glory in!*

*Who is this king of glory?
Yahweh the strong, the valiant,
Yahweh valiant in battle? (Ps. 24:7).*

As the *Sefer Torah* is taken out the benediction is pronounced: "Blessed be he who in his holiness gave the Torah to
his people Israel" (*ADPB*, p. 475).

But what is the significance of the *Sefer Torah*? Why does
this scroll become the center of Jewish life at this moment in
all the communities of Palestine, in the Diaspora, in the synagogue of Nazareth, as well as in the Temple of Jerusalem?

To the Jew of that period every object was sacred, every
human act had religious meaning. But the *Sefer Torah* is
unique, as it is the whole Pentateuch written on a scroll of
parchment. Reading it each week reenacts the great moment in

history which occurred on Mount Sinai; it was therefore fitting that all the holy rites surrounding it be multiplied and that the attitudes and gestures of all those who approached it be appropriate to the greatness of this moment.

The rabbinical tradition at the time of Jesus obliged each Jew to copy the Pentateuch for his personal use once in his lifetime. Thus is interpreted the passage in Deuteronomy 31:19: "Now write down this song which you must use; teach it to the sons of Israel."

A Jew who is not able to write the scroll himself must ask a scribe to copy it for him. If he inherits a scroll, he is still obliged to write one or to have one written. The Talmud forbids selling it even in cases of dire need. Yet in very exceptional circumstances, to defray the expenses of one's wedding, for instance, it may be sold.

The *Sefer Torah*, which is intended for reading in public, must be written on the skin of a pure animal, whether a quadruped or a bird. A stiletto is used in writing it, and the best black ink with a soot base. The text must be inscribed in the square (cuneiform) Hebraic characters.

It is the duty of the scribe to prepare himself by silent meditation for that holy task. He must have before him a copy of the Pentateuch which has been corrected and verified. The scribe must refer to it continuously and never write a word from his own memory or without first pronouncing it aloud. Special care must be taken in writing the divine names. Before each of these the scribe must pronounce the formula: "I intend to write the holy Name." If he forgets one single time, the scroll is unfit to be read in public. It must be entirely rewritten.

When the scribe has started to write the name of God, he must not stop until he has finished. Whoever passes by a scroll must kiss the material that covers it. A scroll must never be kept in a bedroom, and if it is damaged or worn, it must be placed in a room set aside for safekeeping; that room is called *gueniza*. The alternative disposition of a used scroll is to place it in an earthen jar which is later to be laid in the coffin of a man who has devoted his life to the study of the Law.

The *Sefer Torah*, thus surrounded with respect and adoration, is not a book like any other, to be placed in a bookcase, set apart from life. It represents the living Law which at all important moments in the life of Israel must inform the actions of the community. In the days of the kings, the monarch owned two copies, and one of them remained near his throne at all times but in time of war accompanied him to the field of battle.

Each Saturday morning, the sacred scroll is taken out and carried in procession around the synagogue before being placed on the platform. All the faithful come close, holding the end of their *tallith*, with which they touch the book; they then kiss the part of their prayer shawls which has come into contact with the Torah.

The leader now holds the scroll in his hand. First, he faces the tabernacle and then turns towards the congregation, raising the book high as he presents it for the veneration of the faithful. As he does so he recites a short passage of the *Shema*: "Hear, O Israel: the Lord is our God, the Lord is One. Great is our Lord; holy is his Name. Magnify the Lord with me, and let us exalt his Name together" (*ADPB*, p. 481).

Having then placed the scroll on the *tebah* at the center of the platform, the minister begins to unroll the *Sefer Torah* until he comes to the passage that is to be read that day. When these rites are completed, the minister calls one by one those who will have the honor of saying the blessings on the holy book before the reading of the day. The person thus chosen to read, who may be any member of the congregation, says a blessing : "Bless ye the Lord who is to be blessed."

And the congregation responds: "Blessed be the Lord, who is to be blessed for ever and ever."

The reader continues aloud: "Blessed art thou, O Lord our God, King of the universe, who hast chosen us from all peoples, and hast given us thy Torah. Blessed art thou, Lord, giver of the Torah" (*ADPB*, pp. 485, 487).

The leader then begins the reading of the *Parashah*, the reading for that Sabbath from the Pentateuch. Theoretically, it
must be read in Hebrew, the language of prayer, the language
of God. Yet, as some faithful may have little knowledge of the
sacred idiom, it often happened in Jesus' time that each verse
was read first in Hebrew and then in the vernacular, that is, in
Aramaic. Aramaic, a Semitic language close to Hebrew without having the same priestly function, was undoubtedly the
language used by Jesus in his everyday life. Several Aramaic
expressions can be found in the Gospels. When, for example,
Jesus spoke to Jairus' daughter, ordering her to rise from the
dead, he said in Aramaic: *Talitha, kum*! which means "Little girl,
I tell you to get up" (Mk. 5:41). When from the cross Jesus cried
out, "My God, my God, why have you deserted me?" he spoke
again in Aramaic: *"Eli, Eli, lama sabachthani"* (Mt. 27:46).

When the reading of the passage was completed, the reader
pronounced the final blessing which was an elaboration on the
blessing he had said at the beginning:

> *Blessed art thou, O Lord our God, King of the universe, who
> hast given us the Law of truth, and hast planted everlasting
> life in our midst. Blessed art thou, O Lord, giver of the Torah
> (ADPB, p. 191).*

This ritual was repeated as each passage from the book was
read, each time that one of the faithful was called "to the
Torah" to share the honor of reading the sacred text.

After the reading of the Law the sacred scroll was unrolled,
raised and shown to the congregation who bowed as they
repeated:

> *And this is the Torah which Moses set before the children of
> Israel, according to the commandment of the Lord by the hand
> of Moses. It is a tree of life to them that grasp it, and of them
> that uphold it everyone is rendered happy. Its ways are ways
> of pleasantness, and all its paths are peace. The length of days
> is in its right hand; in its left hand are riches and honor. It*

*pleased the Lord, for his righteousness' sake, to magnify the
Law and to glorify it (Ibid., p. 193).*

The reading of the law, the *Parashah*, was followed by the
Haftorah, a passage from the Prophets. The ritual of the *Haftorah*, though more recent than that of the Pentateuch, was
nevertheless in use before the Christian era. Therefore the
young Jesus was familiar with it and took part in it. Another
scroll was unfolded on the *tebah*. Although of great holiness,
this text is not directly from God, as is the Torah.

The teaching of Israel always includes two parts: first, the
Torah, the Bible, and second, the commentaries. God appeals
to human intelligence or reason to adapt his message to the
particular circumstances in the life of his people. This is why
the *Haftorah* succeeds the *Parashah*.

When the rabbi has ended the prophetic reading, he utters
the final blessing which marks the end of this part of the
worship and the replacing of the *Sefer Torah* in the tabernacle.

*For the Torah, for the divine service, for the prophets, and for
this Sabbath day, which thou, O Lord our God, hast given us
for holiness and for rest, for honor and for glory,—for all
these we thank and bless thee, O Lord our God, blessed be thy
Name by the mouth of every living being continually and for-
ever. Blessed art thou, O Lord, who hallowest the Sabbath
(ADPB, pp. 497, 499).*

Such was the climax of the weekly Saturday morning service. Although there are many allusions to that ritual in the
Gospels and in the Acts of the Apostles, it is impossible to tell
exactly which part of the Pentateuch was read on any particular Sabbath in Jesus' time, especially because the entire *Sefer
Torah* was read in cycles varying from one to four and a half
years.

But if we are thinking of the last Sabbath service which
Jesus and his family attended at Nazareth before leaving for
Jerusalem to celebrate the Passover, perhaps we may guess

which part of the Pentateuch was read publicly, or at least was
studied during the meditations of the Sabbath day.

Since Passover, *Pesach*, was the annual commemoration of
the exodus from Egypt and of the liberation of the Hebrews, it
is likely that at the time of Jesus the reading of the Torah,
whether public or private, was from that part of Exodus which
tells of this event: the last verses of chapter 13 and chapter 14.
It is possible that on the Sabbath that preceded Passover, the
story was read which told of the events that led up to the
Exodus, of the pressure God exerted on Pharaoh to allow the
Hebrews to go. Considering the political circumstances in the
Palestine of Jesus' day, this story must have had special interest. Here is one of the main episodes, which was certainly
read:

> *Yahweh said to Moses, "Stretch out your hand towards
> heaven so that hail may fall on the whole land of Egypt, on
> man and beast and all that grows in the fields in the land of
> Egypt." Moses stretched out his staff towards heaven, and
> Yahweh thundered and rained down hail. Lightning struck
> the earth. Yahweh rained down hail on the land of Egypt. The
> hail fell, and lightning flashing in the midst of it, a greater
> storm of hail than had ever been known in Egypt since it first
> became a nation. Throughout the land of Egypt the hail struck
> down everything in the fields, man and beast. It struck all the
> crops in the fields, and it shattered every tree in the fields.
> Only in the land of Goshen where the Hebrews lived, was
> there no hail.*

> *Pharaoh sent for Moses and Aaron. "This time," he said, "I
> admit my fault. Yahweh is in the right; I and my subjects are
> in the wrong. Entreat Yahweh to stop the thunder and the
> hail; I promise to let you go, and you shall stay here no
> longer."*

> *Moses answered him, "The moment I leave the city I will
> stretch out my hands to Yahweh. The thunder will stop, and
> there will be no more hail, so that you may know that the*

> *earth belongs to Yahweh. But as for you and your courtiers, I*
> *know very well that you have no fear yet of Yahweh our*
> *God." The flax and the barley were ruined, since the barley*
> *was in the ear and the flax budding. The wheat and the spelt,*
> *being late crops, were not destroyed.*
>
> *Moses left Pharaoh and went out of the city. He stretched*
> *out his hands to Yahweh and the thunder and the hail stopped*
> *and the rain no longer poured down on the earth. When*
> *Pharaoh saw that rain and hail and thunder had stopped, he*
> *sinned yet again. He became adamant, he and his courtiers.*
> *The heart of Pharaoh was stubborn and, as Yahweh had fore-*
> *told through Moses, he did not let the sons of Israel go (Ex.*
> *9:22-35).*

This fragment of *Parashah* was translated into Aramaic at a
time when Israel was once more under the yoke of a foreign
and idolatrous people, the Romans. It comforted the congregation as in more recent times it has comforted Jews who are un-
dergoing other persecutions. To Jesus, the *Parashah* was not
only characteristic of his people's destiny, but a foreshadowing of his own, a destiny which was to face sin, resistance
and rejection by many of his contemporaries.

And when, just before the replacing of the sacred scrolls in
the tabernacle, the blessing resounds: "Blessed art thou, O
Lord, giver of the Torah," he may have had an intimation that
this splendid gift of God, transmitted to every thirteen-year-
old Jewish boy, carries with it both glory and a burden of
struggle and suffering. Does he foresee all that he will himself
experience?

We can not only guess what section of the Pentateuch was
read just before he left for Jerusalem, a kind of forewarning of
the trials that were in store for him, but we can also guess
what text from the Prophets he heard, one that may have
suggested to him the extraordinary mission that would be his.

For it is a passage from Malachi which is read on the Sabbath preceding Passover, one which announces the coming of

the Messiah. It can, of course, be interpreted in different ways, but it is certainly one of the passages that connect Jesus with Jewish spirituality.

> ... Since the days of your ancestors you have evaded my statutes and not observed them. Return to me and I will return to you, says Yahweh Sabaoth. ... This is what those who fear Yahweh used to say to one another. But Yahweh took note and heard them: a book of remembrance was written in his presence recording those who fear him and take refuge in his name. On the day which I am preparing, says Yahweh Sabaoth, they are going to be my own special possession. I will make allowances for them as a man makes allowances for the son who obeys him. Then once again you will see the difference between an upright man and a wicked one, between the one who serves God and the one who does not serve him. For the day is coming now, burning like a furnace; and all the arrogant and the evil-doers will be like stubble. The day that is coming is going to burn them up, says Yahweh Sabaoth, leaving them neither root nor stalk. But for you who fear my name, the sun of righteousness will shine out with healing in its rays; you will leap like calves going out to pasture. You will trample on the wicked, who will be like ashes under your feet on the day I am preparing, says Yahweh Sabaoth. Remember the Law of my servant Moses to whom at Horeb I prescribed laws and customs for the whole of Israel. Know that I am going to send you Elijah the prophet before my day comes, that great and terrible day. He shall turn the hearts of fathers towards their children and the hearts of children towards their fathers, lest I come and strike the land with a curse (Ml. 3:7, 16-24).

The scrolls of the Law and the Prophets are then placed near the *tebah*, and the service ends with the prayers that mark the climax of the Jewish liturgy. We have quoted some from the Friday evening service, such as the *Oleynu* and the *Kaddish*; others belong only to the Saturday morning liturgy. Such is the priestly blessing:

> *Our God and God of our fathers, bless us with the threefold*
> *blessing of thy Torah written by the hand of Moses thy ser-*
> *vant . . . the Lord bless thee and keep thee! The Lord make his*
> *face to shine upon thee, and be gracious unto thee! The Lord*
> *turn his face unto thee, and give thee peace!* (ADPB, p. 155).

Then the prayer for the faithful assembled:

> *May he who blessed our fathers, Abraham, Isaac and Jacob,*
> *bless all this holy congregation, together with all other holy*
> *congregations . . . those also who unite to form Synagogues*
> *for prayer, and those who enter therein to pray . . . may he*
> *remove from them all sickness, heal all their body, forgive all*
> *their iniquity, and send blessing and prosperity upon all the*
> *work of their hands, as well as upon all Israel, their brethren;*
> *and let us say, Amen* (ADPB, pp. 503, 505).

And finally the *Kedusha*:

> *We will sanctify thy Name, even as they sanctify it in the*
> *highest heavens, as it is written by the hand of thy prophet:*
> *and they called one unto the other and said: Holy, holy, holy,*
> *is the Lord of hosts, the whole earth is full of his*
> *glory. . . . The Lord shall reign forever, thy God, O Zion, unto*
> *all generations. Praise ye the Lord* (ADPB, pp. 453, 455).

The *Kedusha* will become, almost word for word, part of the
Christian liturgy, *Kadosh, kadosh, kadosh*, becoming *Sanctus,
sanctus, sanctus*.

Before leaving for Jerusalem to face the elders who will be
judges of his religious maturity, Jesus, in this last ceremony in
Nazareth, has experienced again the deep spirituality of Israel.
He and his parents have entered into an intimate relationship
with their Creator and have exulted at the thought of actively
contributing to his glory. The blessings they have uttered were
their loving recognition of the Law given by God. They shared
the divine teaching of Sinai as well as the human commentaries inspired by him which adapt that teaching to the contin-

uous unfolding of history. Jesus may well have been aware that he was to be a decisive factor in the history of Israel, and especially in that day when, facing the pagan world, it would have to renew and reform its proclamation of its God-given message.

He does not yet see how his mission and that of his disciples will develop, but he is already conscious of all he owes to the millennia of Jewish life in which he is but a "moment."

3. Journey to Jerusalem

"O LORD MY GOD and God of my fathers, vouchsafe to help me in this journey."

These are the opening words in the traditional ritual used by travellers at the outset of a pilgrimage. Mary, Joseph and Jesus surely took part in it as they left for Jerusalem.

These pilgrimages to the holy city were then a regular part of Jewish life. Every male Jew was obliged to go to the Temple three times a year (Ex. 23:14;Dt. 16:16): for Passover, Pentecost and the Feast of Tabernacles. Although women and children were not obliged to go, they usually accompanied the men, as on other occasions of worship. "Call the people together, men, women, children, and the stranger who lives with you, for them to hear it and learn to fear Yahweh your God and keep and observe all the words of this Law" (Dt. 31:12).

To encourage pilgrimages, all kinds of facilities were planned along the way. Roads leading to Jerusalem were repaired, and wells dug. During the thirty days preceding the holiday it was forbidden to hire professional mourners to wail over the dead; the money set aside for the journey to Jerusalem was not to be spent on their salaries. The innkeepers of Jerusalem were required to lodge pilgrims free of charge — their sole compensation being the skins of animals killed at the sacrifices. Often, of course, pilgrims were welcomed in private homes. They were specially favored also in that the priests allowed them to see the "shewbread" which was normally locked in the sanctuary for their own use. These loaves, twelve in number like the tribes of Israel, reminded one of the gratitude he owed God for his food.

On the tenth day of *Nisan* at Nazareth in the early afternoon, the pilgrims have gathered to set out for the Temple at Jerusalem. They are conscious of the solemnity of the occasion. They have donned the traditional dress and have taken provisions for a four-day journey. Each has a few cakes for the road and a few coins secured in his headdress or in his belt. If he has enough money to ride a donkey, he wears two tunics to protect himself from the cold. If he walks, he carries a stick, the stick of the poor, and wears simple thin-soled sandals held by leather thongs.

The ritual prayers include one which recalls the journey of the patriarch Jacob, and two Psalms. Here is the beginning of this prayer in its modern form, if not literally the same, the same in essence:

> *May it be thy will, O Lord my God and God of my fathers, to conduct me in peace, to direct my steps in peace, to uphold me in peace, and to lead me in life, joy and peace unto the haven of my desire. O deliver me from every enemy, ambush and hurt by the way, and from all afflictions that visit and trouble the world. Send a blessing upon the work of my hands. Let me obtain grace, loving kindness and mercy in thine eyes and in the eyes of all who behold me. Hearken to the voice of my supplications; for thou art a God who hearkenest unto prayer and supplication. Blessed art thou, O Lord, who hearkenest unto prayer (ADPB, p. 1045).*

> *No disaster can overtake you,*
> *no plague come near your tent:*
> *he will put you in his angels' charge*
> *to guard you wherever you go (Ps. 91:10-11).*

Next comes the recalling of the journey of the patriarch:

> *And Jacob went on his way, and the angels of God met him.*
> *And when Jacob saw them, he said, "This is the camp of*
> *God." And he called the name of that place* Mahanaim *,Gn.*
> *32:1-3). . . . Behold, I send an angel before thee, to keep thee*
> *by the way, and to bring thee into the place which I have*
> *prepared (Ex. 23:20). . . . The Lord bless thee, and keep thee:*
> *the Lord make his face to shine upon thee, and be gracious*
> *unto thee: the Lord turn his face unto thee, and give thee*
> *peace (Nb. 6:24-26).*

Thus comforted by the memory of Jacob, the faithful conclude their prayer:

> *Thou art my shelter; thou wilt preserve me from trouble;*
> *thou wilt compass me about with songs of deli-*
> *verance. . . . The Lord of hosts is with us: the God of Jacob is*
> *our stronghold. O Lord of hosts, happy is the man that trus-*
> *teth in thee. Save, Lord: may the King answer us on the day*
> *when we call (ADPB, p. 1045).*

All the pilgrims now chant the verses of two psalms related to their journey:

> *If you live in the shelter of Elyon*
> *and make your home in the shadow of Shaddai,*
> *you can say to Yahweh, "My refuge, my fortress,*
> *my God in whom I trust!"*
>
> *He rescues you from the snares*
> *of fowlers hoping to destroy you;*
> *he covers you with his feathers,*
> *and you find shelter underneath his wings.*

You need not fear the terrors of night,
the arrow that flies in the daytime,
the plague that stalks in the dark,
the scourge that wreaks havoc in broad daylight.

Though a thousand fall at your side,
ten thousand at your right hand,
you yourself will remain unscathed,
with his faithfulness for shield and buckler.

You have only to look around
to see how the wicked are repaid,
you who can say, "Yahweh my refuge,"
and make Elyon your fortress.

No disaster can overtake you,
no plague come near your tent:
he will put you in his angels' charge
to guard you wherever you go.

They will support you on their hands
in case you hurt your foot against a stone;
you will tread on lion and adder,
trample on savage lions and dragons.

"I rescue all who cling to me,
I protect whoever knows my name,
I answer everyone who invokes me,
I am with them when they are in trouble;
I bring them safety and honour.
I give them life, long and full,
and show them how I can save" (Ps. 91).

I lift my eyes to the mountains:
    where is help to come from?
Help comes to me from Yahweh,
    who made heaven and earth.

No letting our footsteps slip!
  This guard of yours, he does not doze!
The guardian of Israel
  does not doze or sleep.

Yahweh guards you, shades you.
  With Yahweh at your right hand
sun cannot strike you down by day,
  nor moon at night.

Yahweh guards you from harm,
  he guards your lives,
he guards you leaving, coming back,
  now and for always (Ps. 121).

The pilgrims covered the eighty-eight miles from Nazareth to Jerusalem in four days. As they passed through the changing landscape they filled the hours with blessings, prayers and reflections on the destiny of Israel. Sometimes the burning issue of the coming of the Messiah was taken up in a low voice: is he coming soon, or has he already come? They discussed Daniel's prophecy that the Messiah would come after a seventy weeks' wait (Dn. 9:24), or that of Hillel, who held that the Messiah had come at the time of Hezekiah. These conversations gave the travellers a chance to display their knowledge of the sacred texts.

The first day the pilgrims travelled from Nazareth to Beth-Shan, the center of a rich and well-developed region. "If paradise is to be found in Palestine, the door to it is Beth-Shan," wrote a Talmudist. Its olives and the linen clothes that were made there were a source of pride to the people and were even mentioned in the Talmud. Therefore, during this first stage of the journey, the travellers said ritual blessings to thank the Lord for the bounty and charms of nature.

When they passed a fragrant tree or bush, the pilgrims said: "Blessed art thou, O Lord our God, King of the universe, who createst fragrant plants" (*ADPB*, p. 989).

When on their way they enjoyed the scent of an aromatic plant or fruit, they said another blessing: "Blessed art thou, O Lord our God, King of the universe, who createst fragrant woods" (*Ibid.*).

When they saw trees in bloom they praised God for all the good things of earth: "Blessed art thou, O Lord our God, King of the universe, who hast made thy world lacking in nought, but hast produced therein goodly creatures and goodly trees wherewith to give delight unto the children of men" (*Ibid.*, p. 991).

As they approached the city, they first pronounced the blessing fitting to good news: "Blessed art thou, O Lord our God, King of the universe, who art good and dispensest good" (*Ibid.*, p. 993), and another, more definite, for the entrance into Beth-Shan.

That city, however, posed problems for the pilgrims and especially for Jesus, who had left Nazareth for the first time. At Beth-Shan there was, of course, a Jewish community faithful to the observance of the Law, which welcomed the pilgrims on that first evening. But there was also an important Roman colony which had established pagan customs in the town. The pilgrims had to be careful. They were forbidden to look at statues of Bacchus erected in the household courtyards and at the temples consecrated to idols. Nor were they to eat impure meats, prepared otherwise than prescribed by the Torah. It was very likely at Beth-Shan that Jesus encountered the pagan world for the first time and came face to face with Roman civilization.

The next two days: ". . . With the mountains of Judah on either side, they followed the Jordan Valley which ran straight south to the Dead Sea. The road skirted a bald mountain on one side; on the other side of the valley, another mountain just as bleak stretched out indefinitely. Between them the Jordan flowed, when it flowed. The further the pilgrims walked, the hotter and heavier the air became, for the valley which slopes steadily downward, finally drops to 1,300 feet below sea level at the place where the Jordan empties into the Dead Sea. There the air is heavy with dust.*

In this wild country where, beginning with early spring, heavy storms trouble the atmosphere, the pilgrims had occasion to say numerous blessings: the blessing on lightning: "Blessed art thou, O Lord our God; King of the universe, who hast made the creation"; on thunder: "Blessed art thou, O Lord our God; King of the universe, whose strength and might fill the world"; finally, on the rainbow, shining when calm prevails once more: "Blessed art thou, O Lord our God, King of the universe, who rememberest the covenant, art faithful to thy covenant and keepest thy promise" (*Ibid.*, p. 991).

On the evening of the third day they came to Jericho, a large and densely populated city, with wide avenues lined with trees and many hotels, bazaars full of the products of the East and markets selling tropical fruits.

On the fourth day, early in the morning, the pilgrims set out on the last stretch, the hardest one, almost seventeen miles long. They had to climb the mountains of Judah rising from 1,300 feet below sea level to an altitude of 2,700 feet. The climb was unbroken and crossed land even more desolate than the valley of the Jordan. But just before reaching Jerusalem, the countryside changed; there were cultivated fields on each side of the road, olive and carobtrees, fields of grain and vineyards. Perhaps Joseph explained to Jesus that the manner of their cultivation consecrated these fields to the Lord. In those belonging to a disciple of Shammai, who was strictly orthodox, one could see spaces three furrows wide between the plantings; in those belonging to a disciple of Hillel, who was more liberal, the intervals were only the width of a yoke.

The fruit trees whose produce were reserved for tithing, that is, for the service of the Temple, were bound with vines and

---

*M. *Marnas*, Miriam, la jeunesse de la Vierge replacée dans son cadre historique (*Paris: Librairie Académique Perrin, 1913*), p. 45.

marked in red letters with the word"sacred." So, as they approached the holy city, the pilgrims must have been impressed by the visible consecration of the surrounding countryside.

After they had reached Bethany and climbed the Mount of Olives they suddenly came in sight of their goal, the holy city, Jerusalem, with the Temple in the foreground.

> How I rejoiced when they said to me,
>   "Let us go to the house of Yahweh!"
> And now our feet are standing
>   in your gateways, Jerusalem (Ps. 122:1-2).

Joseph and Mary show "the House," *Beth*, to the child. The House is the central part of the Temple, deep within which is the Holy of Holies. Behind it rises a secular building with ninety marble towers, the palace of Herod, enclosed by great walls — an imposing white mass of stone which obstructs the horizon and is a reminder of the domination of an often tyrannical power. On the northern side of the city, gardens surrounded by hedges and a few vineyards are the only oases of green in all the conglomeration of houses and palaces. How different this city, both a religious and political center, from Nazareth, which the pilgrims have left only four days ago!

During their last stop on the Mount of Olives before entering the city, Joseph and Mary must have pointed out the Temple to Jesus and shared with him their memories. Joseph recalled the ritual pilgrimages which he had made to fulfill the Law on the occasion of each of the three great holidays celebrated in the Temple. He described also what he might have heard from his parents of the arrival of the Romans and the implanting of paganism in the country.

In the city itself where the Roman presence was brutal and overpowering, the Jewish pilgrims encounter the forces of the occupying power at almost every step. It was they who controlled and regulated their entrance into the holy city, they who watched the interior of the Temple from the Antonia Tower to prevent trouble. And finally and most importantly, it was they who represented the presence of a pagan cult close to the Temple, a cult which one must scrupulously avoid. Is there not a saying of the doctors of Israel to be recorded later in the Talmud that one must shun not only an idol but even "the shadow of an idol"?

The presence of the Romans must have reminded Joseph of some actual events which had shocked him and which he very likely shared with Mary and Jesus. When the Temple was inaugurated, King Herod took precedence at the ceremonies over the High Priest. Although Herod was at least partly Jewish, his politics pursued the interests of Rome. And Titus, governor of Syria, had attended this same ceremony surrounded by his guards flying his colors.

Another happening, even more shocking, had had tragic consequences and lived long in the memory of the Jews. Herod had placed a large golden eagle on the outer door of the Temple, as a blatant reminder of the Roman domination. One night two young men had taken it down and thrown it out of the Temple. To retaliate, Herod had them executed and removed the High Priest Mathias from office, imagining him responsible for the incident. The sight of the Temple must have sharpened these memories of servitude which Joseph surely communicated to his wife and Jesus.

As for Mary, her memories at this impressive moment of arrival were probably of a different kind, more personal, more intimate, and perhaps more likely to impress Jesus. The Christian tradition asserts that Mary had been consecrated to God at birth, a practice which at that time was certainly unusual. Undoubtedly she had been brought up in the observance of the Law, the Prophets and perhaps even of the Doctors of Israel. It is possible that after the death of her parents she had been accepted in one of the religious schools attached to the Temple in the Bezetha district. She may have taken the "Nazirite" vows, a kind of Jewish Third Order which imposed special rules established by Moses himself (Nb. 6): to abstain from fermented drinks, from approaching a dead person and from cutting one's hair.

Whether or not Mary had had this special training and taken these vows, it is certain that because of her ancestry and family ties she had been closely associated with the life of the Temple at Jerusalem. Was it not her cousin, the priest Zechariah, who officiated in the sanctuary? Therefore, she must have remembered being taught by the Doctors of Israel, especially by the Pharisees, whose oral teachings, collected in the Talmud, define what each Jew must accomplish in following the commandments of the Torah: "To observe a precept is of no account," they said, "if one does not practice it according to tradition."

The treatise *Pirkey Aboth* is an example of the loftiness and sense of mystery present in the writings of the synagogue fathers. Here is the opening passage, which Mary may well have read:

> *Moses received the Torah on Sinai, and handed it down to Joshua; Joshua to the elders; the elders to the prophets; and the prophets handed it down to the Men of the Great Assembly. They said three things: Be deliberate in judgment; raise up many disciples; and make a fence round the Torah.*

> *Simon the Just was one of the last survivors of the Great Assembly. He used to say, "Upon three things the world is based: upon the Torah, upon Divine service, and upon the practice of charity."*

> *Antigonos of Socho received the tradition from Simon the Just. He used to say, "Be not like servants who minister to their master upon the condition of receiving a reward; but be like servants who minister to their master without the condition of receiving a reward; and let the fear of Heaven be upon you."*

> *José, the son of Yoezer, of Zeredah, said, "Let thy house be a*

meeting house for the wise; sit amidst the dust of their feet; and drink in their words with thirst."

José, the son of Yochanan, of Jerusalem, said, "Let thy house be open wide; let the poor be members of thy household."

Joshua, the son of Perachyah, said, "Provide thyself a teacher; get thee a companion; and judge all men charitably."

Nittai, the Arbelite, said, "Keep thee far from a bad neighbour; associate not with the wicked; and abandon not the belief in retribution."

Judah, the son on Tabbai, and Simeon, the son of Shatach, received the tradition from the preceding. Judah, the son of Tabbai, said (in the judge's office), "Act not the counsel's part; when the parties to a suit are standing before thee, let them both be regarded by thee as wicked; but when they are departed from thy presence, regard them both as innocent, the verdict having been acquiesced in by them."

*   *   *   *   *

Shemayah said, "Love work; hate lordship; and seek no intimacy with the ruling power."

*   *   *   *   *

Hillel said, "Be of the disciples of Aaron, loving peace and pursuing peace, loving thy fellow creatures, and drawing them near to the Torah."

He used to say, "A name made great is a name destroyed; he who does not increase his knowledge, decreases it; and he who does not study, deserves to die; and he who makes a worldly use of the crown (of the Torah), shall pass away."

*   *   *   *   *

Hillel said, "Separate not thyself from the congregation; trust not in thyself until the day of thy death; judge not thy fellow-

*man until thou art come into his place; and say not anything
which cannot be understood at once, in the hope that it will be
understood in the end; neither say, when I have leisure I will
study; perchance thou wilt have no leisure."*

*   *   *   *   *

*Rabbi Gamaliel used to say, "Do his will as if it were thy will,
that he may do thy will as if it were his will. Nullify thy will
before his will, that he may nullify the will of others before
thy will* . . . (ADPB, pp. 613-633).

These quotations reveal the differing temperaments of the
rabbis. Mary had understood those differences and could pass
on to her son the significance of these judgments in a universe so devoted to the sacred that every human gesture held a
special importance. On the other hand, she may well have
helped him see the excessive rigidity hidden behind the
religious controversies.

What is certain is that Mary also remembers having attended, in the women's gallery, services at which her cousin
Zechariah performed the rites, either at the daily worship or at
the great festivals. She had seen the altar, and on the left of the
altar the bronze font that was used for the sacrifices, and
beyond that the door of the large porch that led to the Holy of
Holies. She had also seen Zechariah standing at the entrance
to the priests' court, his hand resting on the head of the victim. All these impressions which had struck her imagination
as a child she may have shared with her son who was about to
witness the same rites.

There may have been a deeper cause for Mary's emotion as
Jesus was about to accompany her to the sanctuary. Was not
Mary, perhaps in a special way, consecrated to the Lord, and
had her vocation not been constantly and strangely apparent
throughout all the important events of her life? Between these
events and the liturgy of the Temple she had noticed strange
parallels, coincidences and signs, which seemed to suggest

that her life was under the influence of the same spirit which moved through the ceremonies.

Likewise, her son's birth is supposed to have occurred the day after the Feast of *Hanukkah*, which recalls the reconsercration of the Temple after its desecration by Antiochus Epiphanes. She may have had intimations that such coincidences, such parallels between the law and her life as well as the life of Jesus, would continue throughout their lives—Jesus will die the day after Passover. Mary no doubt realizes that these solemn feasts that bring the faithful to Jerusalem, that evoke great moments in the tradition and history of all the people, form the sacred setting in which she and her descendants will live out their destiny. Therefore, she does not feel a stranger in the great Temple she enters, and she knows that from now on her son will also feel at home in this place so familiar to her.

Before going up to the sanctuary, the pilgrims consecrate this moment of intense fervor by singing one of the psalms of *Hallel*, and then reciting a benediction from the *Amidah*. Here are the words of the *Hallel* that rise up to heaven:

Alleluia!

You servants of Yahweh, praise,

praise the name of Yahweh!
Blessed be the name of Yahweh,
henceforth and for ever!
From east to west,
praised be the name of Yahweh!

High over all nations, Yahweh!
His glory transcends the heavens!
Who is like Yahweh our God? —
enthroned so high, he needs to stoop
to see the sky and earth!

> He raises the poor from the dust;
> he lifts the needy from the dunghill
> to give them a place with princes,
> with the princes of his people.
> He enthrones the barren woman in her house
> by making her the happy mother of sons (Ps. 113).

And here is the sixth benediction of the *Amidah*:

> We give thanks unto thee, for thou art the Lord our God and
> the God of our fathers for ever and ever; thou art the Rock of
> our lives, the Shield of our salvation through every genera-
> tion. We will give thanks unto thee and declare thy praise for
> our lives which are committed unto thy hand, and for our
> souls which are in thy charge, and for thy miracles, which are
> daily with us, and for thy wonders and thy benefits, which are
> wrought at all times, evening, morn and noon (ADPB, p. 151).

The pilgrims set out again in the early afternoon; they go
down to the brook of Kidron which flows in the valley skirting
the Mount of Olives. When they reach the other bank they
climb the hill of Moriah upon which the Temple itself is built,
and enter Jerusalem through one of its eastern gates.

The first district they go through is Bézétha where Mary may
have stayed during her years of study. She knows well its narrow, commercial streets, inhabited by merchants of woolens
and hardware, coppersmiths and dealers in old clothing. They
then come to the Pool of Bethesda where most of the pilgrims
take the ritual baths required before entering the Temple. Next
they attend one of the two daily ceremonies in which the sacrifices are offered. The first takes place at nine in the morning
and the other at three in the afternoon—perhaps at the very
time when Jesus finally reaches the end of his journey.

The sacrifice is performed in the open air in front of the
eastern door of the Temple. Eleven priests come in procession
from the northern side, headed by three in sacerdotal robes.
They wear long, narrow tunics, and on their heads, mitres in

the shape of crowns. All are barefooted. The "master of the sacrifice" walks ahead to the left of the altar to purify himself by washing in a bronze ewer. He then returns to the northern side of the priests' court, to the place chosen for the immolation. The lamb is held down by a Levite—one of the descendants of the tribe of Levi—whose duty it is to serve in the Temple and to prepare the ceremonies.

The "master of the sacrifice" lays his hand on the head of the lamb, thus carrying out the rite of *semikath*, whose purpose is to identify the priest with the animal. By this symbolism the life that is poured out to God in the blood is no longer the animal's but that of the man who slays it. This requires that God accept the substitution of the sacrificer for the victim. This is why, as the priest makes ready to slay the animal, the congregation responds with a wish: "May God accept you." Then the sacrificer plunges his knife into the lamb's throat and returns to the altar.

Jesus can see the Levites collecting the blood of the lamb in a basin while others skin it. The blood and the flesh are brought to the sacrificer, who pours a small quantity of blood over the altar, then burns the fat, removing the entrails, and leaving the meat to roast on the altar fire. He then goes towards the Holy of Holies and opens its door with a double key. He enters alone while all the faithful prostrate themselves on the pavement. Within the sanctuary, in great solitude, he accomplishes the final act of identification by sprinkling the blood, swinging the censer and saying a short prayer. This ritual completed, he returns to the courtyard and asks the priests to bless the gathered faithful. To that the Levites answer, "Amen," and one of the priests reads verses of the Decalogue and three sections of the Shema.

Meanwhile the flesh of the lamb has been cooked; some pieces are consumed on the spot by the priests and Levites who have been chosen. The rest is carried away to be eaten by lesser clergy. The whole ceremony lasts a half hour.

For the first time in his life Jesus has now seen the celebration of a sacrifice. The cult of the synagogue at Nazareth
included no such rites. It must be a great moment for him
when he first attends this essential liturgy of the Temple. What
strange new customs these! The "celebrants" are dressed in
ceremonial robes and wear crowns, while at Nazareth everyone, including the celebrant, wears ordinary clothes adorned
only by fringes. Here the celebrants are invested with a
priestly power that isolates and distinguishes them from the
rest of the faithful. At Nazareth any member of the village
community can lead the service and at any point in the ceremony take the part of the rabbi or of the cantor in front of the
tebah. Here in Jerusalem where the officiants are so sharply
distinguished from the congregation, it would not even have
occurred to Jesus that Joseph or any other person could substi-
tute for the celebrant. When he attended the service at
Nazareth he knew that a year after he had gone through his
Bar Mitzvah he would be able to participate in the cult or even
direct it. In Jerusalem, on the contrary, he knows that unless
he takes special vows and becomes part of a hierarchy, he will
never be permitted to serve the Lord in the liturgy.

It may also have surprised him that at the end of the sacrifice one of the priests enters the sanctuary and speaks alone to
God. At Nazareth, as in all the other synagogues and as-
semblies, the whole community participated in the sacred service; one could even say that it was the whole community that
took on the priestly function.

All the differences between what he already knows and
what is suddenly revealed to him suggest to Jesus that the
bloody sacrificial rite which he has just watched, in its origin
and meaning, may be a kind of anomaly, sublime, but some-
how inconsistent with the Jewish religion to which he is accustomed.

What then is the origin, and the symbolic meaning of that
sacrifice?

Originally, the Jewish sacrifice was inspired by similar

pagan rites. In the Old Testament we see that the Canaanite gods were offered sacrifices like those that Yahweh will later be offered in the Temple. The prophets, those vigorous reformers who tried to bring religion back to its original simplicity, protested against such sacrifices. Amos, for instance, points out that the people of Israel did not offer sacrifices in the desert: "Did you bring me sacrifice and oblation in the wilderness for all those forty years, House of Israel?" (Am. 5:25).

Jeremiah stresses this point when Yahweh declares: "What do I care about incense imported from Sheba, or fragrant cane from a distant country? Your holocausts are not acceptable, your sacrifices do not please me" (Jr. 6:20).

Likewise, Hosea: "For I desire steadfast love and not sacrifice, the knowledge of God, rather than burnt offerings"(Ho. 6:6; RSV).

As he watches the sacrifice Jesus may have felt that he was witnessing for the first time a spiritual and historical transformation of the religion of Israel. For the basic idea of the sacrifice, as we have seen, was that the blood poured before the altar became the vehicle for the soul of the sacrificer. Now, according to the Jewish thought of that time, the life of each man consisted of two elements: the *ruach*, or spiritual, corresponding more or less to what we call "soul," and the *basar*, the physical, corresponding more or less to what we call "body." The first of these elements is linked with the blood, the second with the organs.

The libation of the blood and the consumption of the flesh are the two essential parts of sacrifice, the rite of purification, whose primordial function is to eradicate sin. So the body of the animal undergoes a double transformation through the rite of *semikath*: by representing both the soul and the body of the sacrificer it takes upon itself the sins of the spirit as well as those of the flesh. Therefore, if not a magical rite, it is at least an allegorical or symbolical one that Jesus watches, and this may surprise him after the cult to which he has grown accustomed at Nazareth, so realistic, concrete, existential. He had lived until now in the world of blessings. Today he is introduced to another world, the world of sacrifices which in some respects resembles the first but in many others differs from it.

This world is more structured, more legalistic. At Nazareth each prayer, each blessing is an appropriate accompaniment to the natural unfolding of the circumstances of daily life, but the sacrifices represent a gradation from the humble to the most exacting, from the simple to the most complicated.

The rites of expiation and purification are graded as follows:

> a medium-sized lamb is offered for the sins of the faithful;
>
> a large lamb for the sins of priests;
>
> a ewe is offered for the purification of one who has eaten forbidden fat;
>
> a bull is offered by a judge who has made an unjustified decision;
>
> a billy-goat by a teacher who has taught false doctrine;
>
> a ram by a thief, after making restitution;
>
> a sheep by one who has committed a deliberate sin in secret;
>
> a goat by one who has made a simple error.

Besides these sacrifices of purification, there were also those of consecration, the consecration of a high priest by the sacrifice of a young bull burnt outside the sanctuary, for instance.

There was a special sacrifice for the return of lepers into the community. A bird was offered, with which the leper identified himself. Then a second bird was soaked in the blood of the first and released outside the city. As it flew off it supposedly carried away the soul of the leper and all the evil which burdened him. Once the bird had disappeared, the leper was pure and could return to his normal environment.

The Temple with 23,000 Levites divided into twenty-four classes officiating by turns, its 1,500 priests and hundreds of thousands of pilgrims who throng there for Passover, this magnificent Temple dominating the holy city, both exalts and stifles the spirituality of Israel. The synagogue with its family rite was certainly closer to the boy. It was more intimate and more real. There has always been a tendency in Israel to resist clericalism, a conflict between the spontaneity of the family cult and the hierarchy and regulation of the sancturary. As we have already seen, the prophets opposed the ritualistic expression of religious aspiration. Opposition is manifested above all by Korah, one of the most surprising characters of the Bible (Nb. 16).

Korah was a contemporary of Aaron when the latter was made high priest, that is, when professional priesthood was founded in Israel. According to a biblical text and certain commentaries, particularly Rashi's, Korah protested to Moses and said in essence: "God has just proclaimed through your voice that the people of Israel is a sacerdotal people and a nation of priests. So what need is there to establish a priesthood and to choose Aaron for high priest?" In answer Moses referred to the will of the Lord, but Korah, accompanied by two hundred and fifty Hebrews of the same mind, took up arms and rebelled. He was punished: he disappeared with his accomplices as the ground opened up and swallowed them. Then fire rushed before the Lord and consumed the two hundred and fifty men.

Korah failed, but his spirit, the spirit of resistance to professional priesthood, endured in Israel. A commentary on the Talmud declares that in each Jewish generation Korah reappears. Perhaps at the time of Herod and Caiaphas Jesus is the one in whom Korah lives again. As he approaches the Temple, he may remember the rebel who dared struggle against the establishment and died as he did so. Although Jesus is not an activist, there is perhaps in him a little of the spirit of the rebel of Mount Sinai, and in this he would be true to the tradition of Israel. What we do know is that he attends the celebration of a sacrifice for the first time in his life, and passes from the world of blessings to the world of sacrifices.

In spite of prayers and sacred texts common to the synagogue and the Temple, in spite of the ties between them, they
are two different worlds, and Jesus may be disturbed as he
watches a half real, half allegorical phenomenon, a transferral
which he has not encountered before. The blood of the animal
has become another blood, the flesh of the animal has turned
into another flesh. We may wonder what are the reactions of
the boy who will later be the inspiration for another transferral
affecting his own flesh and blood. Is he attracted or horrified at
this sacrifice which transforms and transcends reality? What
does he feel in the presence of the high priest who addresses
God personally and alone, as he himself will address him
later? He has never seen any Jew doing this before. Each one
has always prayed as an integral part, and in the name of the
whole community gathered in prayer.

It must be an intensely serious and disturbing moment for
the young Jesus. He may be stirred by an insight which will
lead to the emergence of Christianity, and permit him and his
disciples to bring the Gentiles to the One God, the God of
Israel.

The world of sacrifices which he enters today is not only exalting and sublime, it is also baffling as it may distort the
primitive Jewish religion of Abraham and the Prophets. Like
all other worlds, it has its high and its low points, its daily
routine and its moments of exceptional intensity carrying with
it the danger of escaping from reality.

The sacrifice performed twice daily is but one example of
what goes on in that world, and Jesus may sense that he will
have to react against it. The following day he will attend the
sacrifice offered for Passover. Later in the fall in the month of
Tishri, he will attend *Yom Kippur*, the Day of Atonement, the
climax of the Jewish religious life, which is accompanied in
Jerusalem with the most transcendental celebration that exists
in the world of sacrifices. Because he has just attended the
immolation of the lamb, he must be subconsciously ready to
accept the immolation of the scapegoat laden with all the sins

of Israel, the object of all the transubstantiations that will be recounted later on.

The sacrifice of *Yom Kippur*, with its ceremonial and almost hysterical fervor, evolved from the daily sacrifice which Jesus has just witnessed. The emotion he has felt at his first encounter with the Temple ceremonies will be deepened on the day of *Tishri*. Therefore it is fitting to describe *Yom Kippur* here, although chronologically it belongs further on.

The sacrifice of *Yom Kippur*, as it is still recorded in the liturgy of these intense and serious days (*yamin noraim*), unfolds as follows after the purification of the high priest preceding the sacrifices: there is, first, the sacrifice of a bull in the Temple, and second, the purification of the people by the death of the scapegoat immolated outside the sanctuary.

The purification of the high priest, as it was practiced at the time of Jesus, is reported with innumerable details which one must know in order to appreciate this liturgical drama in all its fullness.

> . . . *Thou didst desire Levi, the man thou didst love, to minister unto thee, to separate and to consecrate from his stock him that should minister in the Holy of Holies, crowned with the holy mitre, robed, and bearing the* urim, *abiding seven days in the place wherein all is glorious. The faithful ones separated the High Priest one week before the tenth day, according to the law of consecration.*

> *The water of purification was sprinkled upon him to cleanse him, and each day he sprinkled the blood, burnt incense and trimmed the lamps, that he might become accustomed to the sacred service.*

> *Then the wise elders that sat in the gate gathered around him, and they said unto him, "Read aloud the portion of the Law." On the dawn of the ninth day they escorted him to the eastern gate and some of the beautiful sacrifices of the Day of Atonement passed before him. Towards sunset, the meal that*

was prepared for him was frugal, that his sleep might be calm; the aged men of his tribe led him forth to instruct him in taking his hands full of incense, and they charged upon oath to raise the pillar of incense within the Holy of Holies. His flesh trembled, and he shed tears that his zeal should be doubted; they also shed tears, turning aside as they wept; they sought by thoughtful speech in expounding the Law and by reading Holy Writ to keep him wakeful until midnight. With joy, they to whom the first lot fell removed the ashes from the altar; the second lot was cast for the removal of the ashes from the altar of incense and from the lamp; the third lot was cast among fresh priests, for one that should assist at the offering of incense; and for the arrangement of the members of the sacrifice was the fourth lot cast. As the watchman proclaimed the dawn of day, they spread a veil of fine linen to conceal him; he put off his clothes, bathed, and put on the golden garments; he stood and laved his hands and feet, and performed the first part of the rite of the morning continual burnt offering. He appointed another to complete it, while he received the blood and sprinkled it: he then went to burn incense and to trim the lamps, to offer the burnt offering, and to pour out the drink-offering:

. . . Then spread they again the linen veil as at first: he then entered the chamber of Parvah *in the sanctuary; he laved his hands and feet and put off his golden garments. He went forth and bathed, and put on the white garments, and laved his hands and feet. These garments were of fine linen from Pelusium, of the value of eighteen* manim; *most beautiful they were and fit for him that ministered unto the King of glory. The High Priest's bullock was placed between the porch and the altar, facing the west, with its head turned towards the south.*

He drew nigh unto it and, laying his hands upon its head, made confession of his transgressions, concealing naught in his bosom.

And thus did he say: O God, I have sinned, I have committed iniquity, I have transgressed against thee, I and my household; I beseech thee by thy Name, make thou atonement for the sins and for the iniquities and for the transgressions . . . I and my household; as it is written in the Law of thy servant Moses, at thy glorious command "For on this day shall atonement be made for you: from all your sins, before the Lord."

And when the priests and the people that stood in the court heard the glorious and awful Name pronounced out of the mouth of the High Priest, in holiness and in purity, they knelt and prostrated themselves and make acknowledgment, falling on their faces and saying, Blessed be his glorious, sovereign Name for ever and ever.

And he, in awe, prolonged the utterance of the Name, until they that said the blessing had ended it; to whom he said, "Ye shall be clean." And thou, in thy goodness, didst awaken thy mercy and forgavest thy pious servant. . . .

Then came the sacrifices of the bull and the scapegoat:

He went forth to the east of the court, where two he-goats taken of the congregation, were set. They were alike and equal, both in form and height, and stood ready for the atonement to be made for the iniquity of the backsliding daughter. Two lots that were made of gold were thrown together into a casket, from which he drew one lot for the Name most high, and one lot for the rocky steep. He cried with a loud voice, "A sin-offering unto the Lord." They that heard him answered by blessing the Name. He tied a scarlet fillet about the head of the goat to be sent away, and set it towards the place whither it was to be let go.

He passed on and came a second time nigh to his own bullock; he made confession unto our Rock of his iniquity and that of his tribe.

*   *   *   *   *

He took a sharp knife and killed the bullock as ordained; he received the blood in a bowl and gave it unto him that stirred it, to keep it fluid until the time for sprinkling, lest it should become thick and be unfit for the atonement rite. Plucking flaming coals from the altar, he took a light censer wrought of the gold of Parvah, and fashioned with a thin receptable and a long handpiece, and cast three kabs of live coals therein: then they brought him a vessel loaded with the finest beaten incense. He took therefrom his two hands full and put it into a spoon; taking the censer in his right hand and the spoon in his left, he wended his way through the veils and drew near the staves of the ark; he set the censer between the staves and caused the smoke of the incense to ascend; he then came forth. Taking the blood from the priest that stirred it, he returned and stood between the staves. He dipped his finger into the blood and performed the atonement sprinklings; according to the ordained number of times did he sprinkle, once above, and seven times below.

*   *   *   *   *

And thus did he count: one: one and one: one and two: one and three: one and four: one and five: one and six: one and seven.

He came forth and left the vessel upon the pedestal; he killed the goat of the sin-offering, and received its blood in a holy vessel. He retraced his steps and stood in the appointed place before the ark: he performed the sprinklings of the atonement rite according as he did with the blood of the bullock.

And thus did he count: one: one and one: one and two: one and three: one and four: one and five: one and six: one and seven.

He again came without and left the vessel, and took the blood of the bullock: with hastened steps he went and stood outside the veil of separation. He performed the sprinklings before the veil according to the ordinance concerning the cov-

ering, and hastened to perform the sprinklings a second time with the blood of the goat.

He returned to mingle the blood of the two sacrifices wherewith he cleansed the golden altar, sprinkling it seven times upon the pure golden overlay, and putting it upon the four horns.

He hastened and came nigh unto the live goat: then made he confession unto God of the ignorant and presumptuous sins of the people.

*   *   *   *   *

He sent the goat away by the hand of a man that was in readiness unto the rock-bound wilderness, that it should bear the stain of the iniquity of this people unto a solitary land; he drove it over the edge of the rock, and rolling over in its fall, its bones were shattered like the breaking of a potter's vessel. The High Priest took a sharp knife and cut up the bullock and goat of the sin-offerings, and took away the inward parts that were to be burnt upon the altar: and the parts that were to be burnt without the camp did he hang up; he then read aloud the portions of the Law for the day, washed his hands and feet and put off the linen garments; he bathed a third time, put on the golden garments and washed his hands and feet. He took his own ram and the ram of the people and offered them for a burnt offering . . . again he washed his hands and feet, put off the golden garments, bathed and washed his hands and feet, put on the white linen garments and entered the Holy of Holies. He brought out the vessels he had used for the incense, and washed his hands and feet; he then put off the white garments he had worn and put them away for ever: he again bathed, put on the golden garments, and washed his hands and feet: he then offered the continual burnt offering of the afternoon, burnt the incense, and lighted the lamps. The service being then ended, he washed his hands and feet; thus did he bathe five times and washed his hands and feet ten times. Lo! his face was radiant as the sun when he goeth forth in his might, rejoicing as he appeared girded and robed in his gar-

*ments of honour. A perfect people conducted the faithful mes-
senger to his home: they rejoiced at the good tidings, that the
fillet, red as scarlet, had become like snow: they were decked
with salvation and clad with the robe of righteousness: a cry
of triumph rose, as song of joy and gladness. The clouds on
high distilled and dropped their dew; the furrows of the field
ran with water, and the land yielded her increase. They that
gathered in of the seed of peace, gave thanks; they that bare
the sheaves, declared God's praise in melody; the nethermost
parts of the glorious earth gave forth music, and shewed forth
his righteousness to troops travelling by the way. Verily the
messenger had fulfilled the hope of them that sent him: their
hope had come as the cool breeze from a snow-clad land on
the day of harvest. They were washed from their uncleanness,
they were cleared from the taint of their pollution; they
washed their hands in purity, yea, they were made perfect and
whole; to make known that he that cleanseth them is the fountain of living waters; he that purifieth them is the well of
Israel, whose waters never fail. In whiteness and innocence
they were made wholly clean; they were made new, even as
mercy is new every morning; they were cleansed from every
stain; the high praises of God were in their throat, singing was
on their tongue, in their mouth a new song. They rejoice in
dread, and serve in awe the Holy One of Israel, the Sanctifier
of holy beings; they utter joyful song with the timbrel and
cymbal, playing on stringed instruments and singing sweet
psalmody. They cling to the mighty right hand that is exalted
and full of righteousness, and lo! it upholdeth them altogether.
They are drawn near and enter into his gates exulting; joy and
everlasting gladness overtake them on their path. They
triumph and rejoice in his Name all the day; they are made ex-
ceeding glad in his presence.*

*The splendour of their light breaketh forth as the morning;
they lift up their voice, they exult in the majesty of the everlasting Rock. Happy is the people, that is in such a case;
happy is the people, whose God is the Lord* (SOS, II, pp.
160-165).

What effect will this great liturgical feast in the Temple have on the naive and living faith of Jesus? Will it reenforce or confuse the direct approach to God which he and his forebears knew at Nazareth?

Jesus had seen nothing like this in the cult he had known at Nazareth. How deeply all of this must have impressed the young country lad when he first stood before the Temple. He was also conscious for the first time of the presence of the Romans, whose pagan customs perverted the vocation of his country. In fact he would die through a sentence foreign to Jewish Law, the Roman torture of the cross.

In any event, whether or not he felt drawn to these solemnities, his concept of the cult can no longer be the same. Will this new outlook help or hinder his calling? Will it allow him to proceed in the peace of the Lord his God, or will this change be the incipient cause of the political and human drama which ends his mission abruptly, later to be carried on by his followers?

What problems must have emerged whose answers were too numerous and intangible to be grasped at the time! What questions must have burned within the predestined child, questions arising from the two opposing aspects of the tradition of Israel, that of the congregational and of the priestly cults. One can understand why Jesus drew apart from the crowd of pilgrims among whom were his parents to talk with the elders, and to look for answers within himself. One understands, too, why he lingered behind his fellow pilgrims to find peace in prayer and meditation.

He may already have felt that he was moving in a new direction whose goal was unknown. He may have felt divided between the world of blessings and the world of sacrifices. He may have sensed dimly that he was destined to become the lamb of a new sacrifice. It was a crucial moment for him, for Israel and for Christianity.

4. Passover at Jerusalem

WHEN JESUS AND HIS FAMILY reached Jerusalem at the end of their journey, they found it crowded with Jews from all the communities of Palestine and the Diaspora. As the historian Jules Isaac has written of such a time, "one hears every tongue; overflowing crowds swarm everywhere." Fifty years after Christ the historian Flavius Josephus estimated that the pilgrims numbered 2.5 to 3 million. But here again it is not a question of taking the figures literally. It merely is a way of saying that there were huge crowds of people. Actually, there were probably several hundred thousand. Since the normal population of Jerusalem did not exceed 250,000 at that time, the influx of pilgrims would at most have doubled this figure. That meant considerable overcrowding. The pilgrims who had found no lodging in houses camped in the streets or around the city. "To the city of stone is added, in the surrounding countryside, a city of tents."*

---

*Jules Isaac, Jésus et Israel (Paris: Albin Michel, 1948).

In a festive atmosphere which was both national and religious, the Jews assembled in their capital to celebrate, on the one hand, the historic moment of the Exodus, and on the other, a particularly important religious ceremony. It was as if, *mutatis mutandis*, Christmas and Independence Day had been conjoined. The passover that Jerusalem celebrated was perhaps the supreme moment of Jewish life in Palestine, when an ancient tradition going back to earliest times was given new life by the fusion of two celebrations.

> *My father was a wandering Aramean. He went down into Egypt to find refuge there, few in numbers; but there he became a nation, great, mighty, and strong (Dt. 26:5).*

This verse haunted the memory of the Jews gathered in Jerusalem at the time of the Second Temple, as it still haunts many today. But Passover existed in a pastoral form even before the Jews were taken captive in Egypt. It was then a celebration of spring and recalled the creation of the world. As Philo the Jew said: "In those days the elements of nature were distinguished from one another and given harmonious order: the sky was clothed in splendor by the sun, the moon and the course of the heavenly bodies. The earth found its beauty in growing things: whenever rich soil nurtured trees, plants and flowers, they covered hills and valleys with their verdure. And so to remind us of the creation of the world, each year God calls forth a new spring."

Tishri was originally the first month in the secular Jewish calendar, since it was the month of plowing and sowing. *Nisan* was the seventh. But because *Nisan* was associated with the time of renewal and therefore creation, in Jesus' day it had come to be considered the first month of the religious year.

Passover, therefore, like most of the solemn Jewish feasts, originated first in the natural rhythm of the seasons and in the pastoral life of the Aramean nomads who became, after the captivity in Egypt and after Sinai, the first people to worship

One God. Later on, this tradition fused two festivals into one, inserting the historical celebration of Exodus into the liturgy. This is *Pesach*, or Passover itself, the festival of liberation from Egypt and the exodus of the Hebrews on their way towards Mount Sinai and the promised land of Canaan. There was also *Hag-ha-matsoth*, the Festival of Unleavened Bread, the bread which the Hebrews baked for their hasty flight from Egypt.

Thus Jesus and his family found themselves in a religious atmosphere arising from the most ancient pastoral tradition and two striking events in history. They watched the preparations for the feast; they saw huge markets where merchants sold sheep driven down from the neighboring hills, and spices brought by caravan from Mesopotamia. From noon on all work had ceased in the city.

The population and the pilgrims thronged the markets to buy animals either for sacrifice or for food, as well as herbs and spices for the meal of *Seder*. At the beginning of the sacrifice, towards the third hour, the trumpets of the Levites proclaimed throughout the city that the time had come to kill the animals.

Jesus, like all the firstborn in Israel, had been fasting since noon in order to atone through abstinence for the death of the firstborn of Egypt, a death willed by God to force the Pharaoh to let his people go. Soon after the sacrifice he would take part in the Passover meal, which today in Europe is called *Seder*, and which in the Mediterranean communities is called *Haggadah*, because of the traditional text read on that occasion by the head of the family.

Theoretically, this ritual meal must take place in a family setting. A few of the pilgrims who have been welcomed into Jewish homes have shared it with their hosts. Others celebrate it in the streets or in the surrounding countryside, gathering in congenial or regional groups. As Hayyim Schauss has said,

> *Darkness descends on the holy city. Everywhere sheep and goats, spitted on fragrant pomegranate wood, are roasting in the clay stoves which stand in the courtyards of the homes.*

> *These stoves are called Pesach-ovens and are movable; should there be heavy rain they are carried into the house. The groups are now gathering. Relatives and friends assemble from near and from far. Every large room is a meeting place for a group. Nobody is omitted. The poor are invited to the homes of the rich and a spirit of brotherliness, of national unity, binds all together at the feast. All are partners: masters and slaves, men and women, the aged and youthful. All are dressed in white, festive clothes, much adorned and be-decked. . . . In the homes people lounge on sofas placed around the room . . . . First a glass of wine mixed with water is taken . . . . Then the sacrificial animal is served and is eaten with matsoh and bitter herbs, dipped in charoses, a mixture of ground nuts and fruits in wine.**

This Passover ceremony is mentioned several times in the Gospels.

In the Gospel according to Luke it is mentioned twice: first in the account of the journey to Jerusalem to which we have referred, then in the account of the last Passover that Jesus celebrated before the drama of the Passion:

> *Every year his parents used to go to Jerusalem for the feast of the Passover. When he was twelve years old, they went up for the feast as usual. When they were on their way home after the feast, the boy Jesus stayed behind in Jerusalem without his parents knowing it. They assumed he was with the caravan, and it was only after a day's journey that they went to look for him among their relations and acquaintances. When they failed to find him, they went back to Jerusalem looking for him everywhere. Three days later, they found him in the Temple, sitting among the doctors (Lk. 2:41).*

> *When the hour came he took his place at table, and the apostles with him. And he said to them, "I have longed to eat this passover with you before I suffer" (Lk. 22:14).*

---

*Hayyim Schauss, Guide to Jewish Holy Days: History and Observance (*New York: Schocken Books, 1962), p. 54.*

The Gospel according to Matthew also speaks twice of Passover, but both texts refer to the same occasion, namely, Jesus' last Passover. In 26:17, we read of the disciples preparing the meal of the first day of Unleavened Bread, that is, the *Seder*:

> *Now on the first day of Unleavened Bread the disciples came to Jesus to say, "Where do you want us to make the preparations for you to eat the Passover?" "Go to so-and-so in the city," he replied, "and say to him, 'The Master says: My time is near. It is at your house that I am keeping Passover with my disciples.'" The disciples did what Jesus told them and prepared the Passover.*

Chapter 26:30 refers to a verse from the Psalms which constitute the *Hallel*—one of the most important moments in the Passover liturgy.

In the Gospel according to Mark, the beginning of chapter 14 also recalls the Passover and the feast of Unleavened Bread which are celebrated jointly: "It was two days before the Passover. . . ."

In mentioning the approach of Passover, John calls it "the feast of the Jews" which Jesus will celebrate on his arrival in Galilee and also after the resurrection of Lazarus. "It was shortly before the Jewish feast of Passover" (Jn. 6:4). And: "The Jewish Passover drew near, and many of the country people had gone up to Jerusalem to purify themselves" (Jn. 11:55).

And so the festival of springtime, the festival of the liberation from Egypt which periodically marks the life of all Jews, also marked Jesus' life from his childhood to his death.

He first celebrated it during his childhood at Nazareth, where no sacrifice was performed and where, in the course of the family ceremony of *Seder*, he must have played the part of the good child asking questions of his father. At twelve he saw it celebrated at Jerusalem and was to celebrate it throughout his years of adulthood and preaching until the eve of his Passion, which gave to the Jewish Passover and to the meal of *Seder* a new meaning and expression.

The celebration of Passover lasts seven days. First come two full holidays when all work and travel are forbidden; then four partial holidays when work and travel are allowed, ending with a day of strict observance. This division of the Passover week into three distinct periods helps one to understand the timetable of the journey to Jerusalem as recorded by Luke.

The three preliminary days of travel are over on the eve of Passover, at the very moment of the sacrifice which initiates the feast. The two days that follow their arrival at Jerusalem are the two official holidays during which Jesus and the holy family attend the Temple services, and during which the child, now preparing his *Bar Mitzvah*, is questioned by the doctors.

During the four following days, in conformity with both custom and ritual, the return journey to Nazareth should have taken place. But, according to Luke, Mary and Joseph found after their first day of travel that the boy was missing, and they went back to look for him. After three days they found him in the Temple. The four partial holidays intended for their return to Nazareth were, therefore, spent in Jerusalem, as well as the last holy day Jesus, Mary and Joseph would have celebrated together in Nazareth. Luke gives no details as to what took place, but one may suppose that since the last holiday came right after the recovery of the boy, Jesus and his family were obliged to stay in Jerusalem until the end of the week.

The Passover liturgy actually begins with the night preceding it. It begins at the *Seder* meal—which twenty years later will become Jesus' Last Supper preceding his Passion.

The *Seder* meal is one of the most characteristic of Jewish religion, essential to an understanding of the vocation of Israel. On the one hand it is an ordinary meal, since its menu consists of foods which might appear at any meal. In this family gathering around the table, the ritual is composed of a dialogue which seems in its freedom and variety to be a spontaneous conversation animating the meal.

While the *Seder* in its realism seems to treat God like an extra guest welcomed with utter simplicity, it witnesses to the

sacred nature of the world and of life and to the historic vocation of the people of God. Before the food plays its natural part
in sustaining life it is sanctified by benedictions which stress
its sacred nature. By their direct and spontaneous symbolism
they remind one of the vicissitudes that must be endured by a
people chosen for a mission that isolates or distinguishes
them from the rest of humanity. Certain moments of the meal,
certain gestures and words recall the great historic event, the
liberation from Egypt and the crossing of the desert, of which
Pesach is both the reminder and the revival. All this creates an
atmosphere both simple and intriguing, in conformity with
the Jewish concept of a God who intervenes in the world
through natural means. Even miracles, if they occur, do so
without upsetting nature and the world, because they occur at
moments of choice or possibility where an appeal to God may
affect the course of nature but not overthrow it.

Here is a description by Edmond Fleg of the preparation for
the *Seder* at the time of Jesus' first visit to the Temple. The men
don their *yamulkas* as priestly symbol. The symbolic dishes are
already on the table: the egg and roast lamb, horseradish, bitter herbs and *haroseth* — made of apples and crushed almonds;
vinegar and chervil, and *matsoth*, unleavened bread.

The table is made ready for the guests but with one additional place. The prophet Elijah, herald of the Messiah, is expected at the feast, just as he is supposedly present at the time
of circumcision.

Messianism in Israel is lived in perpetual expectation rather
than in the hope of an impending event. Of course the Jews
know that the prophet Elijah will not come to the *Seder*, and
they would be greatly surprised to find at the end of the meal
traces of food on his plate or drink in his cup. But that does
not prevent their waiting for him and hoping for his coming.
His anticipated presence at the time of a meal will show the
young Jesus that the Messianic hope never dies, even when
the Messiah does not appear.

The Passover meal begins like an ordinary one. As the head

of the family takes his place at table he blesses the wine, and everyone then drinks a first cup. During the *Seder* three additional cups of wine will be taken, according to the instructions of the Sages, to commemorate the liberation of the people of Israel (*Mishnah Pesahim*, 10:8). Each of these acts has a special meaning and is preceded by a blessing which sets it in the framework of the ritual.

The first cup is used for *Kiddush*, marking the solemnity of the feast.

The second accompanies the *Haggadah*, the recital of the flight from Egypt.

The third accompanies the thanksgiving at the end of the meal.

The fourth accompanies the *Hallel*, Psalms of gratitude which close the family ceremony on this solemn night, symbolic in so many ways of every man's destiny.

> *I will offer libations to my saviour,*
> *invoking the name of Yahweh.*
>
> *(I will pay what I vowed to Yahweh;*
> *may his whole nation be present!)*

—*Ps. 116:13-14.*

In fact, several times tradition relates these four cups to the four phases of deliverance quoted in the Torah when God promised Moses to free Israel from slavery: "I will free you of the burdens which the Egyptians lay on you. I will release you from slavery to them, and with my arm outstretched and my strokes of power I will deliver you. I will adopt you as my own people" (Ex. 6:6).

After the first cup of wine the head of the family washes his hands, as is required several times during the day. He omits the usual blessing, reserving it for the later ablutions of all those present at the moments in the meal more characteristic of Passover.

Then, as could happen at any ordinary meal, the chervil or the parsley is dipped in salted water or in vinegar with the words: "Blessed is he who created the fruit of the earth." The herbs so seasoned are eaten—this being the first allusion to the bitterness of life which is often the lot of Israel.

After this the unleavened bread is shared, but one piece of it is wrapped in a napkin and hidden under a cushion until the end of the meal, when it is eaten with dessert.

These opening rites are in no way exceptional, nor do they of themselves indicate the solemnity of this meal. But then a ritual dialogue begins among those present to recall the historic event of Passover. The *Haggadah*, the story of the liberation from Egypt, is begun. The head of the family takes the leading part while the youngest child, the "good" child, asks questions which are supposed to express his childish surprise.

The Passover meal is thus a family ceremony at which children are instructed. The dialogue of the *Haggadah* is a mixture of the solemn and the familiar, utter simplicity and true greatness. To begin the ritual dialogue, the father shows the others a piece of unleavened bread:

> *This is the bread of affliction which our ancestors ate in the land of Egypt: let all those who are hungry, enter and eat thereof; and all who are in distress, come and celebrate the Passover. This year we are servants here, but next year we hope to be freemen in the land of Israel.*

The youngest present, the good child, then asks the following questions:

> *Wherefore is this night distinguished from all other nights? Any other night we may eat either leavened or unleavened bread, but on this night only unleavened bread; all other nights we may eat any species of herbs, but this night only bitter herbs; all other nights we do not dip even once, but on this night twice; all other nights we eat and drink either sitting or reclined, but on this night we all of us recline.*

The head of the family answers by reading the story of the Exodus:

> *Because we were slaves unto Pharaoh in Egypt, and the Eternal, our God, brought us forth thence with a mighty hand and an outstretched arm. And if the Most Holy, blessed be he, had not brought forth our ancestors from Egypt, we and our children and our children's children would still be in bondage to the Pharaohs in Egypt. Therefore, even if we were all of us wise, all of us men of knowledge and understanding, all of us learned in the Law, it nevertheless would be incumbent upon us to speak of the departure from Egypt; and all those who speak of the departure from Egypt are accounted praiseworthy.*

> *Originally, our ancestors were idolators, but at present the Lord hath brought us near to his service; as it is said:*

> *Then Joshua said to all the people: "Yahweh the God of Israel says this, 'In ancient days your ancestors lived beyond the River — such was Terah the father of Abraham and of Nahor — and they served other gods. Then I brought your father Abraham from beyond the River and led him through all the land of Canaan. I increased his descendants and gave him Isaac. To Isaac I gave Jacob and Esau. To Esau I gave the mountain country of Seir as his possession. Jacob and his sons went down into Egypt'" (Jos. 24:2-4).*

> *Blessed be he, who observeth strictly his promise unto Israel. Blessed be the Most Holy who computed the end of captivity, that he might perform what he had promised to our father Abraham at the covenant between the parts, as it is said: "Then Yahweh said to Abram, 'Know this for certain, that your descendants will be exiles in a land not their own, where they will be slaves and oppressed for four hundred years. But I will pass judgement also on the nation that enslaves them and after that they will leave, with many possessions'" (Gn. 15:13-14).*

They all raise the cup, saying:

> *And it is that promise which has been the support of our an-*
> *cestors and of ourselves, for not one only has risen up against*
> *us, but in every generation some have arisen against us to an-*
> *nihilate us, but the Most Holy, blessed be he, always delivered*
> *us out of their hands.*

This is the point at which contemporary custom calls for a dialogue between the father of the family and those present. It is not possible to set a date for the origin of the next text, the *Dayenu*. Verse after verse enumerates the merciful acts of God, and to each of them all respond, *Dayenu* ("it would have been sufficient").

> *If He had slain their first-born, and had not bestowed their*
> *wealth on us,* it would have been sufficient.
>
> *If He had given us their wealth and had not divided the sea*
> *for us,* it would have been sufficient.
>
> *If He had divided the sea for us, and had not made us pass*
> *through on dry land,* it would have been sufficient.
>
> *If He had made us pass through its midst on dry land, and*
> *had not drowned our oppressors in the sea,* it would have
> been sufficient.
>
> *If He had drowned our oppressors in it, and had not*
> *supplied our necessaries in the wilderness during forty years,*
> it would have been sufficient.
>
> *If He had supplied our necessaries in the wilderness during*
> *forty years, and had not fed us with manna,* it would have
> been sufficient.
>
> *If He had fed us with manna, and had not given us the Sab-*
> *bath,* it would have been sufficient.

If He had given us the Sabbath, and had not brought us to Mount Sinai, it would have been sufficient.

If He had brought us near to Mount Sinai, and had not given us the Law, it would have been sufficient.

If He had given us the Law, and had not led us into the land of Israel, it would have been sufficient.

If He had led us into the land of Israel and had not built the Temple, it would have been sufficient.

How much more are we indebted for the manifold bounties which the Omnipresent hath bestowed upon us!

After some exposition and commentary from the Bible concerning the paschal lamb, the unleavened bread and the bitter herbs, the head of the family makes a solemn declaration which has come to be the climactic moment of the *Seder*:

In every generation each individual is bound to regard himself as if he had gone personally forth from Egypt, as it is said, "And on that day you will explain to your son, 'This is because of what Yahweh did for me when I came out of Egypt," (Ex. 13:8-9). Thus it was not our ancestors alone, whom the Most Holy, blessed be He, then redeemed but us also did He redeem with them, as it is said, "And he brought us out from there to lead us into the land he swore to our fathers he would give to us" (Dt. 6:23).

Therefore, we are bound to thank, praise, laud, glorify, extol, honour, bless, exalt, and reverence Him who performed for our fathers, and for us all these miracles. He brought us from slavery to freedom; from sorrow to joy; from mourning to festivity, and from servitude to redemption. Let us therefore sing a new song in his presence. Hallelujah!

So ends the first part of the *Seder*. The meal is then served, with the usual benedictions over the wine and the washing of the hands, and the less usual blessings over the unleavened bread and the bitter herbs. A third cup of wine is then taken while leaning on the left elbow. The cup of the prophet Elijah is filled, and the door is opened, either to allow the messenger of God to appear, or to allow the poor to take their place at the meal.

Finally, after the recitation of Psalms, the prayer of adoration is read, *Nishmat kol haï*, already quoted. The ceremony ends as one drinks the fourth and last cup, again reclining to the left. The *Seder* itself is followed by readings from the Bible and by songs, the most popular of which is the "Song of the Kid," the *Had Gadya*. It was composed in Aramaic, the common language of Palestine in Jesus' day — but only written down long after the time of the Second Temple:

> One only kid, one only kid, which my father bought for two zuzim; one only kid, one only kid.

> And a cat came and devoured the kid, which my father bought for two zuzim; one only kid, one only kid.

> And a dog came and bit the cat, which had devoured the kid, which my father bought for two zuzim; one only kid, one only kid.

> Then a staff came and smote the dog, which had bitten the cat, which had devoured the kid, which my father bought for two zuzim; one only kid, one only kid.

> Then a fire came and burnt the staff, which had smitten the dog, which had bitten the cat, which had devoured the kid, which my father bought for two zuzim; one only kid, one only kid.

> The water came and extinguished the fire, which had burnt the staff, which had smitten the dog, which had bitten the cat, which had devoured the kid, which my father bought for two zuzim; one only kid, one only kid.

Then the ox came and drank the water, which had extinguished the fire, which had burnt the staff, which had smitten the dog, which had bitten the cat, which had devoured the kid, which my father bought for two zuzim; *one only kid, one only kid.*

Then the slaughterer came and slaughtered the ox, which had drunk the water, which had extinguished the fire, which had burnt the staff, which had smitten the dog, which had bitten the cat, which had devoured the kid, which my father bought for two zuzim; *one only kid, one only kid.*

Then the angel of death came and slew the slaughterer, who had slaughtered the ox, which had drunk the water, which had extinguished the fire, which had burnt the staff, which had smitten the dog, which had bitten the cat, which had devoured the kid, which my father bought for two zuzim; *one only kid, one only kid.*

Then came the Most Holy, blessed be He, and slew the angel of death, who had slain the slaughterer, who had slaughtered the ox, which had drunk the water, which had extinguished the fire, which had burnt the staff, which had smitten the dog, which had bitten the cat, which had devoured the kid, which my father bought for two zuzim; *one only kid, one only kid.*

This popular song is not only an exaltation of life since it attacks those who would destroy life, but it is also an allegory of the history of Israel: the dominant empires which through the years have often sought to enslave or destroy Israel, end by being themselves destroyed, while the weakest of nations, represented by the kid (Israel), continues to survive. The kid "which my father bought for two *zuzim*" symbolizes the people of Israel linked to God through the two tablets of the Law.

The Passover liturgy, like that of all Jewish holy days, includes the usual Sabbath prayers, but adds special readings appropriate to the occasion. The first day of the feast is a solemn moment in the religious growth of Jesus. He begins by hearing in a more sumptuous setting, in a more elaborate liturgy, the familiar prayers which are the foundation of every Jewish ceremony. He recites to himself the *Amidah*, a series of benedictions; he takes part in the *Kedusha*, the prayer of sanctification, and in the *Barekhuh*, a solemn hymn of praise; and with his hand over his eyes, he takes part in the proclamation of the *Shema*, the creed of monotheism.

This first service which he attends in the Temple may perhaps have both inspired and unsettled him, as his attention is drawn to certain words and phrases which, as the Gospels reveal, will become embedded in his consciousness and will reappear in the course of his teaching.

For instance, in the *Amidah* it is possible that he was especially struck by the verse announcing redemption through the Messiah: "Blessed art thou, O Lord our God and God of our fathers . . . who in love wilt bring a redeemer to their children's children for thy Name's sake" (*ADPB*, p. 131).

Other blessings introduce themes that Jesus will enlarge upon later on. For instance, on the praising of humility: "Blessed art thou, O Lord, who breakest the enemy and humblest the arrogant," or on the mercy of God towards the poorest of men: "Blessed art thou, O Lord, who coverest the naked."

In other instances, words or expressions themselves will be repeated by Jesus. In the prayer of Moses, words are applied to the gods of the idolaters which Jesus will repeat, in a metaphorical way, to designate unbelievers:

> . . . *their idols* . . .
> *have mouths, but never speak,*
> *eyes, but never see,*
> *ears, but never hear (Ps. 115:4-6).*

The first verses of this Psalm will later be the inspiration for the opening of the "Our Father":

Not by us, Yahweh, not by us,
by you alone is glory deserved,
by your love and your faithfulness (Ps. 115:1).

Finally, in the hymns of David there recurs an expression used also in the prophets, especially Ezekiel, which will become "the Son of Man" with new meaning in the teaching of Christ. These words which at first simply refer to the human condition, become synonymous in the Gospels with Messiah, or even with God.

And so during this first Passover service certain words and ideas take shape which later on will be used by Jesus—seedlings of his teaching planted in his mind at the opening of this Jewish festival.

After preliminary blessings, the commemoration of the liberation from Egypt is begun, using the Canticle of the Red Sea of Moses:

Yahweh I sing: he has covered himself in glory,
horse and rider he has thrown into the sea.
Yahweh is my strength, my song,
he is my salvation.
This is my God, I praise him;
the God of my father, I extol him.

*   *   *   *   *

The chariots and the army of Pharaoh he has hurled into the
  sea;
the pick of his horsemen lie drowned in the Sea of Reeds.
The depths have closed over them;
they have sunk to the bottom like a stone.
Your right hand, Yahweh, shows majestic in power,
your right hand, Yahweh, shatters the enemy.
So great your splendour, you crush your foes;
you unleash your fury, and it devours them like stubble.
A blast from your nostrils and the waters piled high;
the waves stood upright like a dyke:
in the heart of the sea the deeps came together.

*   *   *   *   *

Who among the gods is your like, Yahweh?
Who is your like, majestic in holiness,
terrible in deeds of prowess, worker of wonders?

*   *   *   *   *

By your grace you led the people you redeemed,
by your strength you guided them to your holy house.

*   *   *   *   *

You will bring them and plant them on the
mountain that is your own,
the place you have made your dwelling, Yahweh,
the sanctuary, Yahweh, prepared by your own hands.
Yahweh will be king for ever and ever (Ex. 15:1-2, 4-8, 11-12,
    13, 17-18).

Next, as in all Jewish services, comes the reading of the Law, which has already been described. The *Parashah* of the first day of Passover is taken from the twelfth chapter of Exodus:

> *Moses summoned all the elders of Israel and said to them,*
> *"Go and choose animals from the flock on behalf of your fami-*
> *lies, and kill the Passover victim. Then take a spray of hyssop,*
> *dip it in the blood that is in the basin, and with the blood from*
> *the basin touch the lintel and the two doorposts. Let none of*
> *you venture out of the house till morning. Then, when*
> *Yahweh goes through Egypt to strike it, and sees the blood on*
> *the lintel and on the two doorposts, he will pass over the door*
> *and not allow the destroyer to enter your homes and strike.*
> *You must keep these rules as an ordinance for all time for you*
> *and your children. When you enter the land that Yahweh is*
> *giving you, as he promised, you must keep to this ritual. And*
> *when your children ask you, "What does this ritual mean?"*
> *you will tell them, "It is the sacrifice of the Passover in*
> *honour of Yahweh who passed over the houses of the sons of*
> *Israel in Egypt, and struck Egypt but spared our houses." And*
> *the people bowed down and worshipped. The sons of Israel*
> *then departed, and they obeyed. They carried out the orders*
> *Yahweh had given to Moses and Aaron.*

> *And at midnight Yahweh struck down all the first-born in the land of Egypt . . . and there was a great cry in Egypt, for there was not a house without its dead. And it was night when Pharaoh summoned Moses and Aaron. "Get up," he said "you and the sons of Israel, and get away from my people. Go and offer worship to Yahweh as you have asked. . . ." The Egyptians urged the people to hurry up and leave the land . . . . So the people carried off their dough, still unleavened, on their shoulders, their kneading bowls wrapped in their cloaks.*

> *. . . The time that the sons of Israel had spent in Egypt was four hundred and thirty years. And on the very day the four hundred and thirty years ended, all the array of Yahweh left the land of Egypt. The night, when Yahweh kept vigil to bring them out of the land of Egypt, must be kept as a vigil in honour of Yahweh for all their generations (Ex. 12:21-29, 30-31, 33-34, 40-42).*

The reading from the Prophets, the *Haftorah*, which follows, is taken from *Joshua*, chapter 3. Here are the most significant lines:

> *Joshua said to the people, "Sanctify yourselves for tomorrow, because tomorrow Yahweh will work wonders among you."*

> *Then he said to the priests, "Take up the ark of the covenant, and cross at the head of the people." They took up the ark of the covenant and moved to the front of the people.*

> *Yahweh said to Joshua, "This very day I will begin to make you a great man in the eyes of all Israel, to let them be sure that I am going to be with you even as I was with Moses"* (Jos. 3:5-7).

At Passover as at all great Jewish celebrations, the constant flow of history made itself felt as the foundation of religious experience.

Another *Haftorah* read during Passover week is one of the most impressive passages from the Prophets, the vision of Ezekiel:

> The hand of Yahweh was laid on me, and he carried me away by the spirit of Yahweh and set me down in the middle of a valley, a valley full of bones. He made me walk up and down among them. There were vast quantities of these bones on the ground the whole length of the valley; and they were quite dried up. He said to me, "Son of man, can these bones live?" I said, "You know, Lord Yahweh." He said, "Prophesy over these bones. Say, 'Dry bones, hear the word of Yahweh.' The Lord Yahweh says this to these bones: 'I am now going to make the breath enter you, and you will live. I shall put sinews on you, I shall make flesh grow on you, I shall cover you with skin and give you breath, and you will live; and you will learn that I am Yahweh.' " I prophesied as I had been ordered. While I was prophesying, there was a noise, a sound of clattering; and the bones joined together. I looked, and saw that they were covered with sinews; flesh was growing on them and skin was covering them, but there was no breath in them. He said to me, "Prophesy to the breath; prophesy, son of man. Say to the breath, 'The Lord Yahweh says this: Come from the four winds, breath; breathe on these dead; let them live!' " I prophesied as he had ordered me, and the breath entered them; they came to life again and stood up on their feet, a great, an immense army.

> Then he said, "Son of man, these bones are the whole House of Israel. They keep saying, 'Our bones are dried up, our hope has gone; we are as good as dead.' So prophesy. Say to them, 'The Lord Yahweh says this: I am now going to open your graves; I mean to raise you from your graves, my people, and lead you back to the soil of Israel. And you will know that I am Yahweh, when I open your graves and raise you from your graves, my people. And I shall put my spirit in you, and you will live, and I shall resettle you on your own soil; and you will know that I, Yahweh, have said and done this—it is the Lord Yahweh who speaks' " (Ezk. 37:1-14).

The Passover celebration with all its ceremonial and transcendence must appear to Jesus as a link between heaven and
earth. It holds the promise of a life hereafter while it is at the
same time a glorification of life here below. So each is mentioned. At the reading of the Law, the prayer is: "Sanctify us
by thy commandments, that we may merit the long and
blessed life of the world to come: guard us from evil deeds,
and also from evil hours that visit and afflict this world"
(*ADPB*, p. 479).

Almost in the same breath the last verses of Psalm 115 are
recited:

> *The dead cannot praise Yahweh,*
> *they have gone down to silence;*
> *but we, the living, bless Yahweh*
> *henceforth and evermore.*

This tension between heaven and earth, so necessary to
Israel, but always so fragile and precarious, could easily be
thrown out of balance, and this, Jesus may have sensed in his
early years. Will he turn towards the exaltation and mystery
which so easily excite the masses, or towards an austere realism, far more demanding? Jesus must have been aware of this
dilemma for the first time during the Passover celebration.
Perhaps he will become more aware of it during his conversations with the Doctors of the Law, those specialists in rabbinic
commentary before whom he must appear, like all Jewish boys
of his age preparing for their *Bar Mitzvah*.

These scholars know every word, every symbol in the holy
books. As the scrolls are unrolled, they know exactly where to
find each quotation. All the passages of Scripture are embedded in their memories so that their commentaries become
comparisons between different books of the Bible. They comment on a passage from Exodus with a verse from the Psalms,
for instance, or on a narrative from Numbers with a verse from
Ecclesiastes or the Book of Job.

At the time of Jesus their teaching was exclusively oral; there is no record of their reflections or of their commentaries. But we can be certain that in their minds, trained from an early age to absorb different forms of God's word, nothing was ever lost, and that they transmitted to their disciples the wisdom they had acquired—a wisdom which expanded and became more precise through discussions with their fellow doctors.

It was during intervals in the service that the young boys approached the doctors whom they could see from afar in the Temple court. The younger doctors would stand to teach, while the older ones would sit.

Contemporaneous with the time Jesus first approached these doctors, the great Hillel had died. He had been foremost among them and was known to be especially liberal and broad-minded in his interpretation of the Law. Fortunately, Hillel had followers.

Another famous teacher was the venerable Shammai, whose more legalistic disciples opposed those of Hillel. There were many others whose names have been lost, but we do know that at the time of Jesus the controversy between the two rival schools of thought was carried on in the Temple court, even during Passover week.

The doctors instructed the faithful and their children in what today would be called ethics and morality. There were two fundamental positions: the ritualistic, and the realistic or pragmatic or even existential.

The ritualists based all their thinking on the Scriptures, as exemplified in the strange comment of one of the doctors: "How do I know that day follows night? I know it because I have read it in the Torah."

For the others, especially the disciples of Hillel, the reality of life—human or natural reality—was more important than the observance of texts. This is how they put it: "Forget scriptural matters. Let men do as they will. Tradition is within them." Or else: "Go outside and see what men are doing there."

This dominance of life over the letter, or rather this close association of life with the letter, is a deep and continuing characteristic of Jewish thought; it was spelled out in many directives given by the doctors. These state that it was not enough to read a Psalm as an intellectual exercise, but that one must also be concerned with the material needs of men: "The physical needs of others are my spiritual needs," one of the doctors was fond of saying. Could this be one of the sources of the new commandments of Jesus?

This moral teaching completes rather than contradicts the letter of the sacred texts. It includes comments on life which are full of understanding and consolation. "All those who fall find support. There is no fall that does not come to an end." So the spirit continues to inspire and heal, whatever the circumstances.

There were doctors whose view of sin and virtue was not moralistic in the narrow, ordinary sense of the word. Yet they saw life as a perpetual conflict: "The state of non-sin is not a state of innocence, but a state of perpetual conflict in which one must strive without ceasing to approach the good and the true."

Again, some doctors were impressed by the complexity of the world: "One cannot isolate a question. Reality is always a tangle."

There is, therefore, in the teaching of that time a wisdom which will find an echo years later in the preaching of Jesus. There were, however, those who debated endlessly on the exact application of the Law. In other words, there were not only liberals among the doctors but also strict traditionalists. All day long there was debate on how to apply the Torah to daily life. Sometimes there was so much concern with minutiae that the argument must have seemed to the young inconsequential and petty. But to understand the strictness of the rabbis regarding the application of the Law, we must always remember that, since Sinai, the whole Jewish people had been invested with a priestly mission and that every Jew is a

priest. It is, therefore, no more surprising to see them adhere
to strict rules on food, rest, prayer and so forth, than it is to see
monks adhere to very particular practices which distinguish
them from other men and which would seem inexplicable
without an understanding of their sacred meaning.

Thus the doctors may have discussed in detail in the presence of Jesus the requirement that every Jew recite the *Shema*
at night. At what time should this be done? At what moment
of dusk does day turn into night? Some sought physical cri-
teria: night began at the instant that blue could no longer be
distinguished from white. Easy enough to say, argued others,
but what blue is meant, a vivid or a pale blue? Perhaps at this
point in their discussion they asked the young people's
opinion. Perhaps it was on such an occasion that Jesus, by his
common sense and spirituality, impressed the doctors as Luke
assures us he did.

Other questions were broader in scope. The doctors discussed whether the oath of allegiance to the Roman Emperor
was consistent with Jewish religious feeling. Perhaps it was
in listening to these pros and cons that Jesus conceived his
well-known "Render unto Caesar. . . ." Perhaps it was then
that he first expressed that idea. No wonder that the doctors
marvelled at his wisdom.

But the doctors did not confine themselves to theoretical,
moral or religious discussions of this sort. They often sought
to lighten the sessions of work or of interrogation to which the
young were subjected by turning to the *Haggadah*. At the time
of Jesus the rabbinical tradition was oral and was divided into
two parts. Later it became the two Talmuds. The *Halakah* was
the theoretical and legislative section dealing for the most part
with the observance of the Law and in particular with the ceremony of Passover. The *Haggadah* was more poetic, free and
imaginative.

The *Haggadah* is an elaboration of biblical texts and narra-
tives. Its content is both factual and imaginary, and its purpose is to teach by means of symbolism. Thus, the *Haggadah*

interprets as follows the passage from Exodus which is read in
the synagogues on the Sabbath preceding Passover. It describes the successive refusals of Pharaoh:

> *After this, Moses and Aaron went to Pharaoh and said to*
> *him, "This is what Yahweh, the God of Israel, has said, 'Let*
> *my people go, so that they may keep a feast in the wilderness*
> *in honour of me' " (Ex. 5:1-2).*

Here, according to Rabbi Haya bar Habba, is the version
given in the *Haggadah*:

> *The day on which Moses and Aaron first appeared in the*
> *presence of Pharaoh happened to be the anniversary of the*
> *King. All the kings of the earth came on this occasion to do*
> *homage to Pharaoh and to bring him crowns, for he was the*
> *ruler of the whole world. Now the servants of the King came*
> *and announced that two old men were standing outside asking*
> *to be admitted.*

> *The palace of Pharaoh had 400 doors, 100 on each*
> *side. . . . At each gate there were lions and bears, and other*
> *ferocious beasts, and no one could enter unless they threw*
> *meat to them. But when Moses and Aaron entered, all the*
> *animals joyously bounded towards him and his brother, gam-*
> *bolling round them like dogs round their masters, and followed*
> *them wherever they went. Moses and Aaron resembled the*
> *ministering angels, their stature was like that of the cedars of*
> *Lebanon, the pupils of their eyes were like the spheres of the*
> *morning star, their beards were like palm branches, and the*
> *radiance of their countenance was like the splendour of the*
> *sun. In his hand Moses held the wonderful sapphire rod upon*
> *which was engraved the divine Tetragram.*

> *Great was the awe of all present, and the kings took off*
> *their crowns and prostrated themselves before Moses and*
> *Aaron. Pharaoh sat and waited for the two to speak. "Per-*
> *chance they have brought me gifts or a crown," thought he.*
> *But they did not even bow before him.*

"Who are you," he queried, *"and what is your request?"*

"We are the messengers of the Most High, blessed be his Name."

"And what do you want?"

They answered: "Thus speaks the Lord, God of Israel: Let my people go. . . ."

When Pharaoh heard these words, he waxed wroth and said: "Who is your God that I should listen unto him? Hath he sent me a crown or a present? Ye have only come to me with words! I know not your God, and I will not grant his request." Thereupon Pharaoh ordered the chronicles to be fetched from the royal archives so as to find out whether the name of the God of the Hebrews was recorded among the names of the gods of other nations. And the scribe read unto him: "The God of Moab, the God of Ammon, the God of Zidon, . . ."

And Pharaoh said:

"I do not find the name of your God in my books."

On the basis of this imaginative rendering by the *Haggadah* of the historical episode, yet another doctor, Rabbi Levi, has in his turn given the following commentary:

There was once a priest whose servant was a fool. When this priest left the country, his servant went in search of him in the cemetery, crying to all comers: "Have you seen my master?" "Who is your master?" they asked. "Rabbi So and So. . . ." They answered him: "What a fool you are! Does one look for a priest in a cemetery?"

So Moses and Aaron answered the Pharaoh: "O fool, does one look for the living among the dead? All the gods you mention are dead, but our God is the living God and the King of the Universe."

Pharaoh said: "Tell me, is he young or old? How old is he? How many cities hath he captured? How many countries hath he made subject to himself? How long is it since he ascended his throne?"

And Moses and Aaron replied: "The strength and power of our Lord fill the whole world. He was before the world was created, and he will be till the end of days. He created thee and breathed into thee the spirit of life."

"And what is his occupation?" asked Pharaoh, whereto Moses and Aaron replied:

"He stretched out the heavens and laid the foundations of the earth; His voice heweth out flames of fire; he uproots mountains and breaks rocks. His bow is fire, and his arrows are flames. His spear is a torch, his shield a cloud, and his sword a lightning flash. He created the hills and the mountains and covered the earth with grass. He sends down dew and rain upon earth, causes plants to grow, and sustains life. He forms the embryo in the womb of the mother and sends it forth as a living being."

"Ye lie," cried Pharaoh, "when ye say that your God created me, for I am the master of the Universe and I created myself, and also the River Nile."

Then Pharaoh said unto his wise men: "Have ye ever heard the name of the God of these people?"

And the wise men of Egypt replied: "We have heard of him that he is the son of wise men and the son of ancient kings" (Is. 19:11).

And the King of Egypt said unto Moses: "I know not your God, — who is this God that I should listen unto him?"

The young Jesus may well have acquired from such commentaries the sense that the Scriptures were not closed, that to the sacred texts men could add precepts and fables to fit their own needs and aspirations. Did he foresee, in listening to these doctors, that he himself would follow this tradition, and that inspired by the *Haggadah* he would interpret the Torah in a light that would renew its teaching?

5. High Holy Days

Upon his return from Jerusalem where he had been tested by the doctors, Jesus was considered mature in the faith and ready to take part in the priestly life. Since the giving of the Law at Sinai this life was the vocation of every Jew who carried in his flesh the sign of the covenant of Abraham.

The term now used to designate this solemn event in the life of an adolescent is *Bar Mitzvah*, meaning "son of the commandment," and "man of duty," but this is a recent term which dates from the fourteenth century.

The ancient rabbinic terms, those in use at the time of Jesus' profession of faith at Nazareth, were either *gadol*, that is, big, adult, or *Bar-Onshin*, son of punishment, meaning that from now on he is responsible for his acts, and like all adults, can be punished for his faults.

The pairing of these two words is most significant. It shows that the young initiate to the priesthood will from now on exercise all the powers and carry all the responsibilities of a man.

He is allowed to take vows or consecrate his goods to holy ends. He can and must carry the weight of his own sins, whereas before reaching the age of thirteen he was still identified with his father both in life and in death. A very ancient *Midrash* states that a child can incur death as a result of his father's sins; conversely, he may also rely upon his father's merit until he reaches his *perek*, his maturity.

Therefore, one reaches manhood and enters the priesthood at the same time. The umbilical cord which binds a child to his family ethically and spiritually is cut. When at the synagogue in Nazareth, Jesus, wearing his prayer shawl for the first time, begins to say the blessings, he becomes both priest and man. For in Israel, which represents humanity, one can be a priest only if one is fully a man.

The celebration of a boy's coming of age takes place on the first Sabbath of his fourteenth year. The *Bar-Onshin*, the *gadol*, is called upon to read a section of the Law, the *Parashah*, and then a section from the Prophets, the *Haftorah*. He is, therefore, one of the seven men "called up" to the honors of the Torah.

At that solemn moment when for the first time he publicly reads a passage from the sacred text, his father, standing in the assembly of the faithful, silently utters this important benediction: "Blessed be he who hath freed me from the responsibility for this child " (*ADPB*, p. 491).

His teacher, perhaps the rabbi, perhaps the cantor, perhaps simply one who, loving God, has spent his life in the study of the Law, stands beside him and points out the text on the scroll which is unrolled on the *tebah*. Jesus, as his teacher has taught him, adjusts the intonation of his voice according to the passage he must read. If it is a dramatic story, one which portrays the tragedy of Israel, he stresses its most moving passages. If it is a legal text, one of those from Leviticus or Exodus which specify the practical application of the Mosaic Law, his voice is without inflection, even monotonous. But in any case the chanting is very simple and regular. Such is the spontaneous and living accompaniment to the law of truth.

The rabbi or the lay reader says a few words to solemnize Jesus' entry not only into the covenant of Abraham but also into the destiny of Israel. At his side all the leaders of the village take part in this admission of a young Jew to the priesthood.

As a rabbinical text puts it: "All those who are prominent in the town are invited to pray for him; he bows before them and receives their benediction."

Jesus has reached the decisive age of sanctification, when in order to overcome the faults of human nature, he calls upon the good instinct, *yecer ha-tov*, which is a tendency to good arising from the covenant of Israel with God. In this way he can resist the bad instinct, *yecer ha-ra*, without turning to his father for assistance.

Like Abraham who rejected idolatry and became a worshipper of God, when he reached the age of thirteen Jesus received the spiritual power which will make possible his vocation. This is the significance of Luke's story of the journey to Jerusalem, of the encounter with the doctors and the return to Nazareth.

The scrolls of the Torah, as we have already seen, are taken from the tabernacle and unrolled on the *tebah* in preparation for the reading. But before this reading, the young Jesus is called to the Torah for the first time by these words of the rabbi: "I summon to the honor of the Torah our young brother *ha-gadol*." In response, the choir of the faithful sing these words which are words both of welcome and of installation:

"Let the young man come up! May the Lord strengthen, bless and keep him! Blessed be he who comes in the name of the Lord, we give you the welcome of the house of the Lord."

Jesus then pronounces the customary benedictions that every Saturday accompany the reading of the Law: "Bless ye the Lord, who is to be blessed." The congregation answers: "Blessed be the Lord, who is to be blessed, for ever and ever" (*ADPB*, p. 485).

Then come the two benedictions by which every Jew called to the honor of reading the Law prefaces and concludes his

Parashah. Before the reading: "Blessed art thou, O Lord our God, King of the Universe, who hast chosen us from all peoples, and hast given us thy Torah. Blessed art thou, O Lord, Giver of the Torah" (*ADPB*, p. 487).

After the reading: "Blessed art thou, O Lord our God, King of the Universe, who hast given us the Law of truth, and hast planted everlasting life in our midst. Blessed art thou, O Lord, Giver of the Torah" (*Ibid.*).

Between these two blessings is the reading of the Torah (*Parashah*) and the reading of the Prophets (*Haftorah*). If we could only know what were the texts read partly by Jesus himself when he acceded to the priesthood! But how could we find out? We can only speculate. The Scriptures suggest that Jesus was born at the festival of *Hanukkah*. Therefore, his coming of age would have taken place on the Sabbath nearest to this celebration. With this dating as a starting point, we might guess what were the two texts in the Law and the Prophets. Regarding the *Parashah* nothing is certain since the cycle of readings from the Torah has varied during the course of the centuries and is not, therefore, the same today as it was in Jesus' day. On the other hand, it does seem likely that the *Haftorah*, whose cycle has not been revised so often, could have been the same then as it is today.

We are dealing, therefore, with a text from Zechariah (which will be quoted below). It may strike us with special force and power if indeed Jesus read it himself that day or at least heard it read by another. In its last lines there is an extraordinary verse which anticipates the message of this unique child: "Neither by force nor by violence, but by my Spirit, said the Lord God."

Here then is this passage from the *Haftorah* which Jesus might well have read:

> *Sing and rejoice, O daughter of Zion; for lo, I come and I will dwell in the midst of you, says the Lord. And many nations shall join themselves to the Lord in that day, and shall be my people; and I will dwell in the midst of you, and you shall*

know that the Lord of hosts has sent me to you. And the Lord
will inherit Judah as his portion in the holy land, and will
again choose Jerusalem.

. . . "Hear now, O Joshua the high priest, you and your
friends who sit before you, for they are men of good omen:
behold, I will bring my servant the Branch. For behold, upon
the stone which I have set before Joshua, upon a single stone
with seven facets, I will engrave its inscription, says the Lord
of hosts, and I will remove the guilt of this land in a single
day. In that day, says the Lord of hosts, every one of you will
invite his neighbor under his vine and under his fig tree."

And the angel who talked with me came again, and waked
me, like a man that is wakened out of his sleep. And he
said to me, "What do you see?" I said, "I see, and behold,
a lampstand all of gold, with a bowl on the top of it, and
seven lamps on it, with seven lips on each of the lamps
which are on the top of it. And there are two olive trees by
it, one on the right of the bowl and the other on its left."
And I said to the angel who talked with me, "What are
these, my lord?" Then the angel who talked with me answer-
ed me, "Do you not know what these are?" I said, "No, my
lord." Then he said to me, "This is the word of the Lord to
Zerubbabel: Not by might, nor by power, but by my Spirit,
says the Lord of hosts. What are you, O great mountain?
Before Zerubbabel you shall become a plain, and he shall bring
forward the top stone amid shouts of 'Grace, grace to it!"
(Zc. 2:10-12; 3:8; 4:1-7, RSV).

And so from now on, surrounded by the good wishes of the
whole community, Jesus is a priest, a Jew. From now on he
will have to apply in all its fullness the ordinances of the Law.
Formerly on the Day of Atonement, *Yom Kippur*, he fasted only
half a day, from dusk to the midday meal. Now he will fast
from nightfall to nightfall.

And if the Doctors of Israel judge him capable of it, he will
interpret the prescriptions of the Law or the words of the
prophets. Is not Judaism a school of free inquiry? Is not the

religion of Israel a free platform where men's thoughts are expressed, adding their commentaries to the Law of the Lord from generation to generation?

Jesus has had only a few months to practice his priestly vocation when it is time for the holy days in Israel, the *yamin noraim*, solemn days at the beginning of the month *Tishri*. These ten days span two festivals, *Rosh Hashanah* commemorating the creation of man, and *Yom Kippur*, the Day of Atonement, when each Jew confesses his sins and solemnly carries out his examination of conscience for the new year.

Jesus realizes that among all the days consecrated to the worship of God and to the sanctification of the universe, there are ten which are dedicated, on the threshold of each new year, to the ethical progress of man and to his forgiveness by God. These are the *yamin noraim*, solemn and awesome days, the holy days of the Jewish year.

They recall the history of the creation of man. They are a reenactment of those days in which God created the world. They are holy because they express the graciousness of the perfect Lord who consents to fashion in men a precarious, imperfect but necessary image of himself to reflect his greatness on earth.

Since the Jewish calendar is lunar, the first appearance of the crescent moon on the horizon indicates the beginning of the month. At that moment a series of fires were lit on the hilltops to carry the news to the whole country. But how were these fires built? Long poles of cedar, some reeds, some olive wood and fresh flax were bound in bundles with thread; they were lit on the top of the mountain and waved up and down until a similar fire was lit on the next mountain. This set off a chain of glowing fires from the Mount of Olives to the Mount of Sartaba, from Sartaba to Gerufna, from Gerufna to Haruan, from Haruan to Beth-Baltin, the last of the line, where torches were waved aloft until the whole land was ablaze.

It is not certain that this rite was still practiced at the time of Jesus. As has been noted earlier, during the battles between the Hebrews and the Samaritans the latter had used this method of signalling by fires to falsify in their own interests the heralding of the new month. To avoid such practices, which could profoundly disturb the life of the people of Israel, it was decided instead to use messengers to announce the new moon, that is, the new month and the new year. But either way it is certain that the transmission of lights was still in the minds of the Palestinians and of Jesus.

These holy days of Israel, which start at *Rosh Hashanah* and end at *Yom Kippur*, are among the most intense and moving of the year. Through each of these days the Jew prepares himself for the purification of *Yom Kippur*; by his ritual gestures and by prayer he grows closer to God.

Every morning the *Shofar* is sounded. Its raucous tones attend the cultic gathering of all the children of Israel. The sound of this ram's horn blown by the celebrant is a reminder of the ram Abraham sacrificed to God in place of his son Isaac. It calls the faithful to an extraordinarily demanding examination of conscience: "Awake from your slumbers, ye who have fallen asleep in life, and ponder over your deeds. Remember your Creator and turn back towards him in penitence."

The sounding of the *Shofar* has as its main objectives:

   to herald the coming of the Lord, creator and master of the world;
   to recall the giving of the Law at Sinai;
   to recall Abraham's sacrifice;
   to encourage penitence;
   to kindle the messianic hope;
   to declare the hope of the resurrection of the dead at the blowing of the *Shofar*, the trumpet of the Last Judgment.

According to a poetic comment on the celebration, "the curve of the *Shofar* represents the religious man's humility, its straight line his simplicity."

Jesus, the young *Yeshua ha-gadol*, is for the first time going to take part in a solemn Jewish observance. The whole village is there to celebrate: there are, of course, the "Jews of *Rosh Hashanah*" and the "Jews of *Yom Kippur*," those who like so many today attend the synagogue only at great feasts, but also those of the faithful who take part in the daily traditional prayers. Each Sabbath, these last are present on Friday evening for the preliminary services, as well as on Saturday morning for the reading of the Torah and the Prophets. They are present again at the Saturday evening service which marks the passing of the day consecrated to God and the return to secular living.

And so all Jews, whether punctilious or lax in their religious practice, meet in the synagogue with an increase of fervor during this period of confession and self-examination, during these ten holy days in which each purifies himself.

Rosh Hashanah is the name for the celebration of the new year, or the first and second days of the month of *Tishri*. By special privilege these two days, according to the Talmud, are considered as one long day. Tradition has it that on the first day of *Tishri* the first man was created; that is why, for Jews, this day marks the beginning of the world. *Rosh Hashanah*, which literally means "the beginning" or the "head of the year," is a reminder of the beginning of history.

> *The first day of the seventh month shall be a day of rest for you, a sacred assembly proclaimed with trumpet call. You must not do any heavy work and you must offer a burnt offering to Yahweh (Lv. 23:24; cf. Nb. 29:1).*

In another passage, from Psalm 81: "Sound the new moon *shofar* . . . on our feastday! This is a statute binding on Israel, an ordinance of the God of Jacob" (Ps. 81:3-4).

This festival of *Rosh Hashanah* is held at a set date each year and is announced to the people in a solemn ritual which has a singular importance. According to a widely accepted tradition in Israel, this day was chosen by God from the beginning of the world as the "day of judgment." This day God opens the ledgers of truth; he examines and weighs the works of each

and every man. As Judge supreme of the year gone by, and of
the year to follow, he decides who is to live and who is to die,
who is to prosper and who is to suffer. The sentence is given
on *Rosh Hashanah*, and a week later, on *Yom Kippur*, it is
definitely sealed. Hence, the extraordinary seriousness of these
yamim noraim that intervene. Hence, the extraordinary intensity
of *Yom Kippur*, the last day on which man may, through contrition, still appeal the judgment passed by God.

No one can escape this judgment; no one can elude the decree
passed by the Lord concerning him unless it be through
prayer, through penitence, through confession. All this is at
stake beginning with the day of *Rosh Hashanah* and continuing until *Yom Kippur*. The proclamation of the judgment pronounced at the first day of *Tishri* is postponed until the tenth
day of the month, the ultimate recourse conceded the sinner
by a merciful Lord. Even before the Law was given, even
before justice was established in Israel, God in his mercy
granted us, in advance, a means of escaping our sin and
redeeming our faults. This carries us back to the creation of
man, to the birth of Adam. Thus this day may also be known
as *Yom Haziccaron*, the Day of Memorial.

Adam's birth is remembered on the first of *Tishri*, while the
penitence undertaken by Adam ten days after he succumbed
to temptation and was expelled from the Garden of Eden is
remembered at *Yom Kippur*. From earliest times God, in his
understanding of human nature, resolved to be kind on that
day towards the descendants of the first man, the first sinner,
and to balance his inflexible justice with mercy.

And so, beginning with Genesis with the beginning of time
and of history, the ten days of *Tishri* are inscribed in characters
of fire in the conscience of every man, in the collective conscience of Israel representing humanity. Many times during
the course of the ages this day of the first judgment has been
the occasion of acts of faith of special intensity, turning points
in the history of men who consecrated themselves to God.

On this day, tradition tells us, Sarah, Rebecca and Anna
addressed their prayers to the Lord and their requests were

granted. The arms of the Lord, we are told, are always open to repentance: "I take pleasure, not in the death of a wicked man, but in the turning back of a wicked man who changes his ways to win life" (Ezk. 33:11).

Who has never sinned? Who has ever passed an entire year without sinning? During all the years preceding the initiation of Jesus, were there ever twelve consecutive months during which the book of life opened at the previous *Yom Kippur* did not threaten to close under the weight of sins and denials?

As Jesus takes part for the first time in the service of *Rosh Hashanah* and for the first time, surrounded by his family and the entire population of Nazareth, begins the ten days' examination of conscience that purifies and delivers from the accumulated sin of twelve months, it is possible that these rites of purification take on for him exceptional significance in view of his own coming mission.

Members of the congregation crowding the benches of the synagogue are clothed in their holiday garments and are conscious of a special dignity, that of men exercising their priestly mission at a specially privileged moment. Their feeling might be compared to the feeling of a Catholic priest celebrating Mass on Good Friday or on Christmas Eve.

The synagogue prayers on this day are the usual prayers but stand out in high relief. They are accompanied by other prayers belonging to these solemnities, prayers which are repeated more often and more insistently as the days go by. These are prayers of contrition, prayers imploring God's grace, prayers of confession essential at this time of individual examination of conscience. And so, little by little, the special solemnity and meaning of the *yamim noraim* is felt, as an undercurrent in the flow of habitual prayers. The young Jesus hears once more the prayers to which he is accustomed, but charged with new meaning and growing intensity.

He hears and repeats the usual opening prayers: "How fair are your tents, O Jacob! How fair your dwellings, Israel!" (Nb. 24:5). There follow the appointed psalms whose every word on

this day of special entreaty takes on more than customary pa-
thos and intensity: "God hear my prayer, do not hide from my
petition, give me a hearing, answer me" (Ps. 55:1-2). Then the
hymn: "How I rejoiced when they said to me, 'Let us go to the
house of Yahweh!' " (Ps. 122:1). Then the *Kaddish:* "Magnified
and sanctified be his great Name in the world which he hath
created according to his will. May he establish his kingdom
during your life and during your days, and during the life of
all the house of Israel. . ." (*ADPB*, p. 207).

All the benedictions and prayers that form the uninterrupted flow of the Jewish Sabbath service, Jesus must have
heard and repeated with growing fervor the *Barekhu*, a solemn
benediction of the Lord: "Bless the Lord who only is worthy
of praise"; the *Amidah*, a litany of silent blessings which glorify
the divine Majesty, the first of which is intensified by the
anxiety and hope of the penitents: "Blessed art thou, O Lord
our God and God of our fathers . . . who bestowest loving
kindness, and art Master of all things, who rememberest the
pious deeds of the patriarchs..." (*ADPB*, p. 449).

There is, of course, the *Shema*, the sublime leitmotiv of Jewish worship: "Hear, O Israel, the Lord is our God, the Lord is
One."

The *Decalogue* which opens with God's own declaration of
his ineffable greatness: "I am Yahweh your God who brought
you out of the land of Egypt, out of the house of bondage" (Ex.
20:1-2).

In words already familiar to us, on the eve of the first day of
Tishri after nightfall, the *Shofar* heralds the opening of the festival: "Sound the new moon *shofar* . . . on our feastday! This
is a statue binding on Israel, an ordinance of the God of
Jacob" (Ps. 81:3-4).

A few moments later in the course of the *Amidah*, these
verses occur with special meaning because of *Rosh Hashanah:*

> *Remember us unto life, O King who delightest in life, and
> inscribe us in the book of life, for thine own sake, O living*

> *God. . . . Grant peace, welfare, blessing, grace, loving
> kindness and mercy unto us and to all Israel, thy peo-
> ple . . . . May it be good in thy sight to bless thy people Israel
> at all times and in every hour with thy peace (ADPB, pp. 133,
> 155).*

Finally, when the service is over, before leaving, the people
exchange good wishes for the coming year: *Leshera tova tika-
tevu,* "May you be inscribed for a happy year."

The following day is the first of the holy days, the first act in
the sacred drama that will determine for a year each man's
destiny. Because of this the tone of the service begins to
change; its direction becomes clearer. First there is a passage
from the *Mishnah* in the earliest rabbinic tradition, which is
part of the daily service and which lists the essential duties
that man must carry out, and whose omission brings punishment.

> *These are the commandments which have no fixed measure:
> the corners of the field, the first fruits, the offerings brought on
> appearing before the Lord at the three festivals, the practice of
> charity and the study of the Torah. These are the things of
> which a man enjoys the fruits in this world, while the stock
> remains for him for the world to come: viz., honouring father
> and mother, deeds of loving kindness, timely attendance at the
> house of study morning and evening, hospitality to wayfarers,
> visiting the sick, dowering the bride, attending the dead to the
> grave, devotion in prayer, and making peace between man
> and his fellow; but the study of the Torah leadeth to them all
> (Mishnah, Peah 1; ADPB, pp. 15, 16).*

After this enumeration of personal and corporate duties, the
service of *Rosh Hashanah* continues with more Psalms than
usual: those which are read daily and those reserved for the
Saturday morning service. There are no less than twelve. Their
verses, sung antiphonally by the leader (facing the tabernacle)
and the congregation, show the greatness and the goodness of

the Judge before whom one has to appear. The very first verses of these texts of adoration express the central theme of the feast: the homage of the Jew to his Creator:

> *Give thanks to Yahweh, call his name aloud,*
> *proclaim his deeds to the peoples!*

*   *   *   *   *

> *He is Yahweh our God,*
> *his authority is over all the earth.*
> *Remember his covenant for ever,*
> *his word of command for a thousand*
> *generations . . . (Ps. 105:1, 7-8).*

> *The heavens declare the glory of God,*
> *the vault of heaven proclaims his handiwork;*
> *day discourses of it to day,*
> *night to night hands on the knowledge.*

> *No utterance at all, no speech,*
> *no sound that anyone can hear;*
> *yet their voice goes out through all the earth,*
> *and their message to the ends of the world.*

*   *   *   *   *

> *The Law of Yahweh is perfect,*
> *new life for the soul;*
> *the decree of Yahweh is trustworthy,*
> *wisdom for the simple.*

*   *   *   *   *

> *Wash out my hidden faults.*

> *And from pride preserve your servant,*
> *never let it dominate me.*
> *So shall I be above reproach,*
> *free from grave sin.*

> May the words of my mouth always find favour,
>   and the whispering of my heart,
> in your presence, Yahweh,
>   my Rock, my Redeemer! (Ps. 19:1-4, 7, 12-14).

Then comes the Psalm of David:

> I will bless Yahweh at all times,
> his praise shall be on my lips continually;

> *   *   *   *   *

> Come, my sons, listen to me,
> I will teach you the fear of Yahweh.
> Which of you wants to live to the full,
> who loves long life and enjoyment of prosperity?

> Malice must be banished from your tongue,
> deceitful conversation from your lips;
> never yield to evil, practice good,
> seek peace, pursue it.

> The face of Yahweh frowns on evil men,
> to wipe their memory from the earth;
> the eyes of Yahweh are turned towards the virtuous,
> his ears to their cry.

> They cry for help and Yahweh hears
> and rescues them from all their troubles;
> Yahweh is near to the broken-hearted,
> he helps those whose spirit is crushed.

> *   *   *   *   *

> . . . Yahweh himself ransoms the souls of his servants,
> and those who take shelter in him have nothing to pay (Ps.
> 34:1, 11-18, 22).

Two themes are woven into these three Psalms: divine greatness and divine justice. In the prayer of Moses, man of God, there is a definite allusion to the approaching judgment:

> *You brush men away like waking dreams,*
> *they are like grass*
> *sprouting and flowering in the morning,*
> *withered and dry before dusk.*
>
> *We too are burnt up by your anger*
> *and terrified by your fury;*
> *having summoned up our sins*
> *you inspect our secrets by your own light.*
>
> *   *   *   *   *
>
> *Relent, Yahweh! . . .*
> *Take pity on your servants! (Ps. 90:5-8, 13).*

And in Psalm 147 the psalmist states that "Yahweh is interested only in those who fear him, in those who rely on his love" (Ps. 147:11).

And so these lyric Psalms which glorify the Lord prepare the way for his coming in judgment. But these phrases, genuflections of the soul, are only a few in the flood of sacred texts inspired by the works of the Creator through which man will worship and adore during the entire year.

The service continues with passages full of anxiety and hope which express man's apprehension as the fearful moment of judgment draws near. Unfortunately we have only late versions of these texts. The first is full of historic allusions:

> *The terrible day of visitation is come, and dread hath seized*
> *all flesh; assembled and with bended knee they raise their*
> *thoughts aloft, even as a whole-burnt offering. O thou who*
> *hast formed man's frame, when thou judgest him and in the*
> *balance weighest both rich and poor, remember the suppliant*
> *prayer of him who said, "Shall not the Judge of all the earth*

*do right?" While yet naught was fashioned, thou didst design
a monument hewn as of rock, steadfast amidst the dawn of
ages and the years untold, a pattern graven for men to look
upon. With sap of youth didst thou enrich her who was his
portion (Sarah) to put forth . . . a glorious branch, a marvellous token to the Lily (Israel), that they might pass into thy
Presence on this New Year's Day. Her offspring tremble,
standing now before thine awful throne, raising their chas-
tened voice in fervent prayer; they throng thy courts, and
with the trumpet they sound an alarm that redemption may be
theirs. They pray in unison and, hastening to thy gates, repose
upon the merit of her (Sarah) to whom thou didst promise visitation. They are supported by the memory of his ashes who
was bound like a lamb (Isaac), of him who was the gift of thy
visitation (SOS, Vol II, p. 96).*

The second describes the day that is approaching:

*The King who reigneth over all the earth wished to found it
upon justice. The world will know all its inhabitants from one
end of the earth to the other will know, that the Creator of the
world does right. When he arises to judge his creatures, to
deliver the oppressed and to destroy the tyrants, a great
silence will reign over all as he casts the wicked from the ends
of the earth. Then a voice will be heard in the heavens and on
the earth: "Lord, how glorious is thy Name in all the world!"*

*His kingdom extends throughout the universe, the depths of
the earth proclaim it, the heavens rejoice in it, the earth
shouts for joy, and the heavens and the seas sing the triumph
of the Lord "whose majesty fills the world, whose kingship
gladdens the earth." On the day of the last judgment the Lord
will cause the shofar to sound three times to shake the power-
ful; he will cast down tyrants from their throne, and all that
breathe will cry out: "How glorious is thy Name in all the
earth!" The Lord will give to the earth pure and lasting joy;
he will revive those who sleep the sleep of death. And songs
will arise: "Sing the praise of the sovereign Lord of the earth."*

The earth and those who dwell therein await with fear and trembling the day of judgment, for that day is great and terrible; and who could claim to be pure in it? Those who exercise justice and those who are conversant with the whole Law, just as those who are called before the Judge, do not know whether they will obtain grace at that hour of judgment. None are favoured before the supreme Judge, for he is no respecter of persons. Each is witness against himself; each signs with his own hands the warrant for his arrest; each is judged by his own deeds. Even the stones of the wall and the beams of the roof give their witness at the time of judgment. Then all will be made true, all will be made just; then justice and mercy will go hand in hand. This is the day when the nations will be called before the supreme Judge. This day is for the judgment of all peoples, of all mortal flesh, in order to recall the first day of creation and to anticipate the last day when all shall be judged (cf. ibid., pp. 104 ff).

Finally, the service comes to an end with the blowing of the *Shofar*, the recalling of the birth of the world, and the heralding of the judgment:

This day the world was called into being: this day thou causest all the creatures of the Universe to stand in judgment as children or as servants. If as children, have pity upon us as a father pitieth his children; and if as servants, our eyes wait on thee until thou be gracious unto us and bring forth our judgment as the light, O God, awesome and holy (ADPB, p. 875, note).

Thou rememberest what was wrought from eternity, and art mindful of all that hath been formed from of old: before thee all secrets are revealed and the multitude of hidden things from the beginning; for there is no forgetfulness before the throne of thy glory, nor is there aught hidden from thine eyes. Thou rememberest every deed, and no creature is concealed from thee: all things are manifest and known unto thee, O Lord our God, who lookest and seest to the end of all generations. For thou wilt bring on the appointed time of memorial when

every spirit and soul shall be visited, and the multitudinous
works be remembered with the countless throng of thy crea-
tures. From the beginning didst thou make this known, and
from aforetime didst thou reveal it. This day, on which was
the beginning of thy work, is a memorial of the first day; for it
is a statute for Israel, an ordinance of the God of Jacob. There-
on sentence is pronounced upon countries—which of them is
destined to the sword and which to peace, which to famine
and which to plenty; and every creature is visited thereon,
and recorded for life or for death. Who is not visited on such a
day as this? For the remembrance of every creature cometh
before thee, man's deeds and destiny, his works and ways, the
thoughts and designs of man and the workings of his imagina-
tion. Happy is the man who forgetteth thee not, and the son of
man who strengtheneth himself in thee; for they that seek thee
shall never stumble, neither shall they ever be put to shame
who trust in thee. For the remembrance of all works cometh
before thee, and thou searchest into the doings of them all
(ADPB, p. 877).

For each holy day, a special Psalm is assigned which usually
is part of the weekly services and which adds to the benedictions its praise exalting the sovereign Judge. On the first day of
the week it is Psalm 24: "To Yahweh belong earth and all it
holds, the world and all who live in it" (Ps. 24:1-2).

The second day, Psalm 48 is chanted. It opens with: "Yahweh
is great and supremely to be praised in the city of our God,"
and ends with: ". . . God is here, our God and leader, for ever
and ever" (Ps. 48:1, 14).

Psalm 82, which is chanted on the third day, concerns justice
and the judgment. It begins with, "God stands in the divine
assembly, among the judges he dispenses justice . . ." and
ends: "Rise, God, dispense justice throughout the world, since
no nation is excluded from your ownership" (Ps. 82:1, 8).

On the fourth day, Psalm 94 calls down God's justice on the
guilty:

> *Yahweh, God of revenge,*
> *God of revenge, appear!*

> *Rise, judge of the world,*
> *give the proud their deserts!*
>
> *Yahweh, how much longer are the wicked,*
> *how much longer are the wicked to triumph? (Ps. 94:1-3).*

The fifth day, Psalm 81 is reminiscent of the sounding of the *Shofar*:

> *Shout for joy to honour God our strength,*
> *shout to acclaim the God of Jacob!*
>
> *Start the music, sound the drum,*
> *the melodious lyre and the harp;*
> *sound the New Moon trumpet,*
> *at the full moon, on our feastday! (Ps. 81:1-3).*

The sixth day, Psalm 93, is one of the briefest but also one of the most fervent in the adoration of God:

> *Yahweh is king, robed in majesty,*
> *Yahweh is robed in power,*
> *he wears it like a belt.*
>
> *You have made the world firm, unshakeable (Ps. 93:1-2).*

Finally, on the seventh day there is Psalm 92, a hymn for the Sabbath, for the world to come which will be all Sabbath and all repose, life and joy eternal. This Psalm of exaltation portrays the universe and mankind delivered from all evil, purified as after the celebration of a final *Yom Kippur*.

> *It is good to give thanks to Yahweh,*
> *to play in honour of your name, Most High,*
> *to proclaim your love at daybreak*
> *and your faithfulness all through the night*
> *to the music of the zither and lyre,*
> *to the rippling of the harp.*

> *I am happy, Yahweh, at what you have done;*
> *at your achievements I joyfully exclaim,*
> *"Great are your achievements, Yahweh,*
> *immensely deep your thoughts!" (Ps. 92:1-5).*

And so from day to day the judgment of God approaches, the fateful end when each will appear face to face before the divine will to receive the recompense for his good or evil actions, to be inscribed in the book of life or in the book of death. This is *Yom Kippur*, the day of judgment, the day of expiation. No longer is contrition expressed in short verses or isolated prayers. Every individual appears before his Creator and joins in the collective examination of conscience, in litanies and innumerable petitions corresponding to the many occasions of sin.

As each one recites the litanies and is made aware of the transgressions for which he must implore the Lord's mercy, he also recognizes his partnership with the Lord in preserving the harmony of the universe. He acknowledges the extent to which he has fulfilled or failed that partnership. These litanies paint an extensive picture of the failings of the human heart.

We shall quote them in their entirety as Jesus probably repeated them. Perhaps it was through them that he gained greater knowledge of the nature of man whose salvation he would seek.

This Jewish liturgy of *Yom Kippur* is both realistic and sublime:

> *Our God and God of our fathers, let our prayer come before thee; hide not thyself from our supplication, for we are not so arrogant and hardened that we should say before thee, O Lord our God and God of our fathers, we are righteous and are sinless; but verily, we have sinned.*

> *We are are guilt-laden: we have been faithless, we have robbed, and we have spoken basely; we have committed iniquity, and caused unrighteousness; we have been presump-*

tuous, done violence, framed falsehood; we have counselled evil, we have failed in promise, we have scoffed, revolted and blasphemed; we have been rebellious, we have acted perversely, we have transgressed, oppressed, and been stiffnecked; we have done wickedly, we have corrupted ourselves and committed abomination; we have gone astray, and we have led astray.

We have turned aside from thy commandments and good judgments, and it availed us nought. But thou art righteous in all that is come upon us; for thou hast acted truthfully, but we have wrought unrighteousness.

What shall we say before thee, O thou who dwellest on high, and what shall we recount unto thee, thou who abidest in the heavens? dost thou not know all things, both the hidden and the revealed?

Thou knowest the secrets of eternity and the most hidden mysteries of all living. Thou searchest the innermost recesses, and dost test the feelings and the heart. Nought is concealed from thee, or hidden from thine eyes.

May it then be thy will, O Lord our God and God of our fathers, to forgive us for all our sins, to pardon us for all our iniquities, and to grant us remission for all our transgressions.

> *For the sin which we have committed before thee under compulsion, or of our own will;*
> *And for the sin which we have committed before thee in hardening of the heart:*
> *For the sin which we have committed before thee out of ignorance;*
> *And for the sin which we have committed before thee with utterance of the lips:*
> *For the sin which we have committed before thee by unchastity;*
> *And for the sin which we have committed before thee openly and secretly:*

*For the sin which we have committed before thee by
deliberate deceit:*
*And for the sin which we have committed before thee in
speech;*
*For the sin which we have committed before thee by
wronging our neighbour;*
*And for the sin which we have committed before thee by
the sinful meditating of the heart:*
*For the sin which we have committed before thee by
association with impurity;*
*And for the sin which we have committed before thee by
confession with the mouth alone:*
*For the sin which we have committed before thee by
despising parents and teachers;*
*And for the sin which we have committed before thee
presumptuously or in error:*
*For the sin which we have committed before thee by
violence;*
*And for the sin which we have committed before thee by
the profanation of the Divine Name:*
*For the sin which we have committed before thee by
impurity of lips;*
*And for the sin which we have committed before thee by
folly of the mouth:*
*For the sin which we have committed before thee by the
evil inclination;*
*And for the sin which we have committed before thee
wittingly or unwittingly:*
*For all these, O God of forgiveness, forgive us, pardon
us, grant us remission (ADPB, pp. 907-913).*

*   *   *   *   *

And also for the sins for which we owe a burnt offering:
And for the sins for which we owe a sin offering:
*And for the sins for which we owe an offering, varying
according to our means:*
*And for the sins for which we owe an offering, whether
for certain or for doubtful trespass.*
*And for the sins for which we are liable to the penalty
of chastisement.*

And for the sins for which we are liable to the penalty
  of forty stripes:
And for the sins for which we are liable to the penalty
  of death by the hand of heaven:
And for the sins for which we are liable to the penalty
  of excision and childlessness:
For all these, O God of forgiveness, forgive us, pardon
  us, grant us remission.

And also for the sins for which we are liable to any of the
four death penalties inflicted by the court, — stoning, burning,
beheading, and strangling; for the violation of affirmative, or
for the violation of negative precepts, whether these latter do,
or do not, admit of a remedy by the subsequent fulfilment of
an affirmative command; for all our sins, whether they be or
be not manifest to us. Such sins as are manifest to us, we have
already declared and confessed unto thee; while such as are
not manifest unto us, are manifest and known unto thee,
according to the word that hath been spoken, "The secret
things belong unto the Lord our God; but the things that are
revealed belong unto us and to our children for ever, that we
may do all the words of this Torah" (Dt. 29: 29). For thou art
the Forgiver of Israel and the Pardoner of the tribes of
Jeshurun in every generation, and beside thee we have no
king, who pardoneth and forgiveth.

O my God, before I was formed I was nought; and now that
I have been formed, I am but as though I had not been formed.
Dust am I in my life: how much more so in my death. Behold I
am before thee like a vessel filled with shame and confusion. O
may it be thy will, O Lord my God and God of my fathers,
that I may sin no more, and as to the sins I have committed,
purge them away in thine abounding compassion, though not
by means of affliction and sore diseases.

O my God! guard my tongue from evil and my lips from
speaking guile; and to such as curse me let my soul be dumb,
yea, let my soul be unto all as the dust. Open my heart to thy
Torah, and let my soul pursue thy commandments. If any
design evil against me, speedily make their counsel of none

effect, and frustrate their designs. Do it for the sake of thy
Name, do it for the sake of thy power, do it for the sake of thy
holiness, do it for the sake of thy Torah. In order that thy
beloved ones be delivered, O save with thy power, and answer
me. Let the words of my mouth and the meditation of my
heart be acceptable before thee, O Lord, my Rock and my
Redeemer (ADPB, pp. 919-923).

Everything has thus been said on the eve of this dramatic day, but everything will be repeated and stressed on the following day, a day of penitence when for the first time Jesus will observe a complete fast, when together with the other Jews of Nazareth he will spend all the hours from daybreak to nightfall at prayer in the synagogue.

This is an impressive body of prayers which has its moments of special intensity, and others less stirring when the attention may even wander, but we cannot record it all. Let us simply look at the last service of the day, the one that concludes the examination of conscience and the appeal for pardon.

This service of *Neilah* is short, intense, breathless, more so than any of those which contribute to the solemnity of *Yom Kippur*. It takes place at the precise moment when the day begins to wane and the shadows spread over the synagogue.

The time indeed is very short to obtain a favorable verdict, the purpose of *Yom Kippur*. In a few minutes every Jew who has been at prayer since the setting of the sun the evening before will be inscribed, as the New Year begins, either in the book of life or in the book of death; every one of them will face judgment as a righteous man or an evildoer. These are anxious moments. In this increasing urgency to wrest from God the final decision, prayers seem to rush towards their end.

First there is the reminder of the Covenant in which the Lord promised to link his destiny to that of his people. This has been handed down to us in a version written long after the Second Temple:

Remember unto us the covenant of the patriarchs, even as
thou hast said: "And I will remember my covenant with Jacob,

*and also my covenant with Isaac, and also my covenant with
Abraham will I remember; and I will remember the land."
Remember unto us the covenant of our ancestors, as thou has
said: "And I will, for their sakes, remember the covenant of
their ancestors, whom I brought forth out of the land of Egypt
in the sight of the heathen, that I might be their God: I am the
Lord."*

*Do by us as thou hast promised: "And yet for all that, when
they be in the land of their enemies, I will not cast them away,
neither will I abhor them, to destroy them utterly and to break
my covenant with them: for I am the Lord their God."*
*Have mercy upon us and destroy us not, even as it is writ-
ten: "For the Lord thy God is a merciful God: he will not forsake thee, neither will he destroy thee, nor forget the covenant
of thy father which he sware unto them."*

*Bring back our captivity and have compassion upon us, as
it is written: "Then the Lord thy God will turn thy captivity
and have compassion upon thee, and will gather thee from all
the peoples whither the Lord thy God hath scattered thee."*

*Gather our dispersed ones, as it is written: "If any of them
be driven out unto the utmost parts of heaven, from thence
will the Lord thy God gather thee, and from thence will he
fetch thee." . . .*

*O blot out our transgressions for thy sake, as thou hast said:
"I, even I, am he that blotteth out thy transgressions for mine
own sake, and will not remember thy sins." Blot out our
transgressions as a thick cloud and as a mist, as it is written:
"I have blotted out as a thick cloud thy transgressions, and as
a mist thy sins: return unto me; for I have redeemed thee."
Turn thou our sins as white as snow or wool, as it is written:
"Come now, and let us reason together," saith the Lord:
"though your sins be as scarlet, they shall be as white as
snow; though they be red like crimson, they shall be as wool."
Sprinkle clean water upon us and cleanse us, as it is written:
"Then will I sprinkle clean water upon you, and ye shall be
clean; from all your defilements and from all your idols will I*

cleanse you." Atone for our sins on this day and purify us, as it is written: "For on this day shall atonement be made for you to cleanse you: from all your sins before the Lord shall ye be clean."

*   *   *   *   *

Give ear unto our words, O Lord, consider our meditation. Let the words of our mouth and the meditation of our heart be acceptable before thee, O Lord, our Rock and our Redeemer. . . . For in thee, O Lord, do we hope. Thou wilt answer, O Lord our God (SOS, Day of Atonement, Vol. II, pp. 90-92).

Then followed litanies whose petitions succeed one another in ever sharper and swifter cadence. From a kind of recitative they shift abruptly into antiphonal verse calling for clemency. *Sela lanu, mahal lanu, kaper lanu. . .* ("Forgive us, be merciful to us, grant us atonement").

Here is the recitative:

Our God and God of our fathers, forsake us not, nor leave us: cast us not off, nor annul thy covenant with us. Bring us nearer to thy Law, teach us thy commandments, shew us thy ways, incline our hearts to fear thy Name. O circumcise our hearts for thy love, that we may return unto thee in truth, and with a perfect heart. And for thy great Name's sake pardon and forgive our sins, even as it is written in thy holy writings: For thy Name's sake, O Lord, pardon my iniquity; for it is great.

And here are the verses, the *Sela lanu* imploring and almost demanding pardon, and above all stressing the historic union between the people of Israel and the God who has chosen them:

For we are thy people, and thou art our God;
We are thy children and thou art our father.
We are thy servants, and thou art our master;
We are thy congregation and thou our portion.

> We are thine inheritance, thou our lot;
> We are thy flock, thou our shepherd.
> We are thy vineyard, and thou art our keeper;
> We are thy work, and thou our creator.
> We are thy faithful ones: thou art our beloved;
> We are thy chosen: thou art the Lord our God.
> We are thy subjects, thou our King;
> We are thine acknowledged people, thou our
>   acknowledged Lord (Ibid., pp. 232-233).

The climax is still to come, the last prayer of the day and the most exalted: deep and melodious sonorities mixed with guttural sounds culminate in cries to God, the cries which always end *Yom Kippur*. It is the *Ovinu Malkenu*, the last thrust towards the Eternal, the last demand of man, the last recourse before their fate is sealed, a very ancient prayer dating from Rabbi Akiba:

> Our Father, our King! we have sinned before thee.
> Our Father, our King! we have no King but thee.
> Our Father, our King! deal with us for the sake of thy
>   Name.
> Our Father, our King! let a happy year begin for us.
> Our Father, our King! nullify all evil decrees against us.
> Our Father, our King! nullify the designs of those that
>   hate us.
> Our Father, our King! make the counsel of our enemies
>   of none effect.
> Our Father, our King! rid us of every oppressor and
>   adversary.
> Our Father, our King! close the mouths of our
>   adversaries and accusers.
> Our Father, our King! of pestilence and the sword, of
>   famine, captivity and destruction, rid the children of
>   thy covenant.
> Our Father, our King! withhold the plague from thine
>   inheritance.
> Our Father, our King! forgive and pardon all our
>   iniquities.

*Our Father, our King! blot out our transgressions, and
make them pass away from before thine eyes.*

*Our Father, our King! erase in thine abundant mercies
all the records of our guilt.*

*Our Father, our King! bring us back in perfect
repentance unto thee.*

*Our Father, our King! send a perfect healing to the sick
of thy people.*

*Our Father, our King! rend the evil judgment decreed
against us.*

*Our Father, our King! let thy remembrance of us be for
good.*

*Our Father, our King! inscribe us in the book of happy
life.*

*Our Father, our King! seal us in the book of redemption
and salvation.*

*Our Father, our King! seal us in the book of
maintenance and sustenance.*

Our Father, our King! seal us in the book of merit.

*Our Father, our King! seal us in the book of forgiveness
and pardon.*

*Our Father, our King! let salvation soon spring forth for
us.*

*Our Father, our King! raise up the strength of Israel,
thy people.*

*Our Father, our King! raise up the strength of thine
anointed.*

Our Father, our King! fill our hands with thy blessings.

Our Father, our King! fill our storehouses with plenty.

*Our Father, our King! hear our voice, spare us, and
have mercy upon us.*

*Our Father, our King! receive our prayer in mercy and
in favour.*

*Our Father, our King! open the gates of heaven unto
our prayer.*

*Our Father, our King! we pray thee, turn us not back
empty from thy presence.*

Our Father, our King! remember that we are but dust.

*Our Father, our King! let this hour be an hour of mercy
and a time of favour with thee.*

Our Father, our King! have compassion upon us and
upon our children and our infants.

Our Father, our King! do this for the sake of them that
were slain for thy holy Name.

Our Father, our King! do it for the sake of them that
were slaughtered for thy Unity.

Our Father, our King! do it for the sake of them that
went through fire and water for the sanctification of
thy Name.

Our Father, our King! avenge before our eyes the blood
of thy servants that hath been shed.

Our Father, our King! do it for thy sake, if not for ours.

Our Father, our King! do it for thy sake, and save us.

Our Father, our King! do it for the sake of thine
abundant mercies.

Our Father, our King do it for the sake of thy great,
mighty and revered Name by which we are called.

Our Father, our King! be gracious unto us and answer
us, for we have no good works of our own; deal with
us in charity and kindness, and save us (ADPB, *pp.*
163-168).

At last, the final benediction is said. It is the *Barekhu eth*
Adonai hamevorach, "Blessed be the Lord who is to be
blessed." All the prayers have been formulated, all the long-
ings addressed to the Almighty, nothing more is to be asked,
or hoped for or demanded. It remains only to exalt the divine
Majesty, whatever will be his verdict, still hidden in the limbo
of the future. Thus the day comes to a close with an affirmation of Jewish faith, with shouts in praise of the oneness of
God. The celebrant flings towards the tabernacle the sacred
phrases, stressing their moving and exultant power in a tri-
umphant voice. *Shema, Israel, Adonai elohenu, Adonai echad,*
"Hear O Israel, the Lord is our God, the Lord is One."

Next, three times over, he intones the benediction: "Blessed
be his Name whose glorious Kingdom is forever and ever."

Then he repeats seven times, as many times as there are
days in the week, as many days as it took the Lord to create the

universe, the abbreviated *Shema: Adonai hu ha-elohim*! "The Lord, he is God!"

Hardly have these words died away than the piercing sound of the *Shofar* is heard, bringing the day to a close. Just as the shepherds of Israel gather home their wandering lambs, so God gathers his people to himself.

The young Jesus has for the first time taken part in the service, in the individual confession which is one of the characteristics of *Yom Kippur*. He, too, has prayed with a simplicity that springs from the heart the prayers of urgency and hope shared by every Jew at the time of the New Year. No intermediary has come between the believer and God. Nor has there been transference of human aspirations to allegory or mythology.

How different is this from pagan rites which Jesus may have encountered on the journey to Jerusalem! How different also this from the sacrifices of expiation that were celebrated in the Temple by the professional clergy who mediated between the faithful and the One whose name is invoked only in the most secret place of the sanctuary! It may have been there, in the synagogue of Nazareth where the *yamim noraim* have just taken place, that the young Jesus was most deeply impressed by the truth and relevance of atonement, this great manifestation of the monotheism of Israel.

It is interesting to note that while the Gospels record the confrontation between Judaism and emerging Christianity and mention numerous feastdays, rites and prayers of the synagogue in which Jesus found himself in opposition to current religion, yet nowhere is *Yom Kippur* so much as mentioned. There is no indication that Jesus either objected to it or took part in it.* Could this be taken to mean that Jesus felt more at ease in its direct prayer to God than in the mediated religion of the Temple?

---

*In the events recorded in the New Testament the only mention of Yom Kippur is in Acts 27:9. In the Epistle to the Hebrews it is probably referred to, but without mentioning it by name.

Conclusion

REVELATION SEEMS to unfold by stages, stages which span about two thousand years. It is as if the course of time were necessary for a religious movement to be initiated, developed and established.

According to legendary material in Genesis, about two thousand years elapsed between the creation of the world and the birth of Abraham. This was the stage of preparation for monotheism. There followed two thousand further years of purely Jewish monotheism, beginning with Abraham, the father of believers, and ending with Jesus. During these two thousand years it was Israel's vocation to witness to the One God. Its mission was to formulate a moral law, to live by its precepts and to experiment with it in an almost entirely pagan, immoral world. This was an overwhelming task for a small nation which was constantly caught between giant empires. Though indeed it was destined to outlive those empires, it was also destined to be oppressed, dispoiled and even decimated by them. But through it all its fidelity was to that simplest and most majestic religious expression, the *Shema*: "Hear O Israel, the Lord is our God, the Lord is One," and to that most perfect expression of morality, the law of love: "Love your neighbor as yourself."

However, the last centuries of the Jewish period saw the emergence of a new stage, in such phenomena as Hellenistic Judaism, and sects such as the Essenes or the Pharisees. These developments led to another period of two thousand years. The preceding era had begun with Abraham; this one began with Jesus. But just as the previous one had come to an end, with the coming of Jesus, this one could end in our day if we do not respond to the current resistance to the teaching of Christ. The former had been a period of growth and gradual acceptance of monotheism by means of the witness of a small nation; the latter could see the historic extension of monotheism throughout the world, as it spreads to all nations for the sake of total conversion from idolatry.

Although Israel was the matrix of monotheism, it apparently does not wish to recapture that role but chooses rather to remain apart from this great movement. It does not recognize its own children although they adore the same God and carry out his commandments. It does not seem to recognize that in order to spread a faith the dynamic of one's action can no longer be the same as that which was appropriate to the stage of its definition. Instead of sharpness, intransigence and even rigor, there must be tenderness, kindness and an obvious concern to appeal to the heart and soothe its suffering.

Abraham forsook his native country in an adventurous gesture, risking everything for everyone. This beginning was terminated only by the beginning of the Christian era. By then the question of God was no longer open; his existence was no longer in doubt; his unity was no longer questioned. The task was how to spread his dominion over the earth, and that constituted a problem vast enough to fill and inspire two thousand years of human history.

Today, after what one could call the revolution of Abraham

which did away with idols in order to find the true God, and after the revolution of Jesus which spread the good news of the victory of the true God, are there not indications that we are entering another epoch of two thousand years? But the inner dynamic of change which we recognize in Judaism at the end of its own period, and which in Christianity was sufficient to spread throughout all peoples the faith of monotheism, seems now to be drawing in upon itself.

The great question, therefore, is whether the response which creates the next stage in morality and religion will come from within the Judaeo-Christian tradition or from outside it; whether Israel and Christianity will have a part in it or not. Will the new revolution in the minds and hearts of men be a new form of the Covenant, or the total annulment of former covenants?

When one considers the present state of religious evolution *sine ira nec studio*, "without anger or false optimism," one feels that the religious thought of the West is just beginning to unfold. Many things are working together: the magnificent and important work of the Ecumenical Council and the succeeding synod of bishops, the attempts—both cautious and visionary—of Popes John and Paul to close the gap between the Catholic Church and the realities of our time, and to persuade it to abandon its outdated privileges, the resulting stimulus among non-Catholics to do the same, the total ecumenical movement which both anticipated and coincided with the decisions taken in Rome, the solidarity that developed between Christians and Jews and the renewal of Judaism. All these movements are preparing the way for a revolution of spirit which is taking place in our time. But even though this may liberalize religion, it does not sufficiently renew its deep roots, and moreover it fails to adapt it adequately to the needs of today.

These innovations have not yet seriously affected our concept of the sacred, which most certainly should be changed in our time. They merely clean the façades of the sanctuaries in which we pray. They may change the forms of prayer and modernize the liturgy, but they do not affect the deep relationships between man and the universe and between man and God. New approaches to both are needed if we are to recover our religious balance.

To discover such approaches certainly goes beyond the limited scope of this work, which is primarily a collection of ancient prayers. And yet when a great religious movement which has known tremendous growth and has shaped the world, is challenged both from without and from within, one realizes, almost always, that the germ of these conflicts existed at its birth. In its period of expansion these elements were held in check and came to the fore only at a time of decline, of questioning and of confrontation with opposing forces.

Such was the case, for instance, with Marxism, whose present difficulties and rivalries existed in embryo in the conflict experienced by Marx in 1846 at the time of his break with other socialists, especially with Proudhon.

In the same way it is possible to suggest that the present crisis in religious thinking felt so keenly by Christianity stems from its own origins in that critical moment in the history of God's revelation, the hidden years of Jesus, those years of his formation by Jewish prayer and worship.

Such is, in any event, the justification for this book. Unorthodox and incomplete as it is, it may yet throw some light on the debate which began two thousand years ago and which until now has hardly been noticed. This is essentially a debate between two religious views of the world. On the one hand we have the world of benedictions, and on the other, the world of sacrifices. In the first instance the sacred is experienced without intermediary as the indwelling presence of God in the universe. In the second instance the sacred must be transposed and mythologized in order to be grasped.

As we have seen, Jesus began to pray at a time when both these views were represented in Jewish worship. In the synagogue where Jesus was trained, and whose architectural remains are still to be found in the soil of Nazareth, there was a world of benedictions where God was approached without intermediary, where the sacred character of the universe was perceived in a direct relationship with the realities of earth and history. On the other hand, the Temple at Jerusalem represented the world of sacrifices in which reaching God and obtaining his support required that one transfigure reality and infuse with mysticism the acts of daily life. The world of the synagogue is part of existential truth whose meaning we would do well to rediscover; the world of the Temple, on the other hand, constitutes a body of allegories which our time has a tendency to question and even to refute.

And so it does not seem pointless to recall the prayers of the young Jesus. Ancient as they are, they touch a responsive chord in the consciousness of contemporary men. Considering the prestige and the great influence on our thinking of the experimental sciences, can we not say that the problem today is one of realizing the presence of the sacred in the universe, and the influence of the spirit in the midst of the scientific and historical determinism within which we live?

Certainly it is not enough simply to return to the world of benedictions, the world of Judaism at the time of Jesus. It cannot be a model, but it could serve as a stimulus to accept the world as it is without trying to transform it by a naive use of the miraculous and the mystical. It could encourage us to accept ourselves as we are, to accept our bodily structure of flesh and bone, our mental structure of sensation and reason as nothing more than a provisional and perceptible stage between the two unfathomable mysteries of birth and death. This world of benedictions could rid us of false problems and help us to seek the genuine ones. It could rid us of the desire to understand mystery and make it possible for us to live with it.

For the world of benedictions is, after all, this world, our world. And can we not in our day draw nearer to God by drawing him nearer to this world, which, we are told, he has fashioned?